TO:

....................................................................

FROM:

..................................................................

# 100
# devotions
## *for the*
## SINGLE MOM

**ZONDERVAN**®

ZONDERVAN

*100 Devotions for the Single Mom*

Copyright © 2023 Zondervan

Portions of this book were adapted from *365 Devotions for Rest.*

Requests for information should be addressed to:

Zondervan, *3900 Sparks Dr. SE, Grand Rapids, Michigan 49546*

Zondervan titles may be purchased in bulk for educational, business, fundraising, or sales promotional use. For information, please email SpecialMarkets@Zondervan.com.

ISBN 978-0-310-14078-8 (softcover)
ISBN 978-0-310-14079-5 (ebook)
ISBN 978-0-310-14080-1 (audio)

Cover design: Jamie DeBruyn
Interior design: Kristy Edwards

*Printed in the United States of America*
23 24 25 26 27  LBC  5 4 3 2 1

No one needs to tell you how difficult being a single mom can be. Whether you are divorced or widowed, have a co-parent or have always parented solo, are newly single or have been a single parent for a long time, you're trying to carry it all—nurturing your children, managing the household, providing financially for your family. Your days are long, you never can seem to get enough sleep, and you are on call 24-7. No matter your situation, this much is true: you are an amazing mom!

If you're a single mom who feels confident in knowing that you are doing a great job raising your kids, working hard while balancing schedules, taking time for self-care, and growing in your faith, praise God! He rejoices with you. Other single moms need your empathy and encouragement, as well as to see your hopeful example.

If you're a single mom who is discouraged, who feels like she is working so hard but falling short as a mom, who is exhausted, lonely, and struggling—God sees you. And what God sees in you is the love you have for your children, the sacrifices you make each day, and the determination you have to raise happy, healthy kids who will follow

Him. You are always enough, and His love for you is unconditional. When you feel weak, He will be your strength. When you are tired, He wants to teach you how to rest. When you are anxious, He will give you peace. When you are sad, He longs to be your comforter. You can trust your heavenly Father with every need.

These daily devotions are set up to remind you that you're not alone. Each day you'll read a Scripture verse, a devotional, and prayer. Use the ruled lines however you'd like—write down prayers, reflect and write down what's on your mind, make a list of goals, create affirmations, or simply journal about your feelings. May these one hundred devotions encourage and equip you to "not become weary in doing good" (Galatians 6:9) as you raise your precious children.

*"Anyone who belongs to God listens gladly to the words of God."*
JOHN 8:47 NLT

Imagine that you have friends over for dinner and your kitchen is buzzing with noise and activity. There is laughter, the clinking of silverware on dinner plates, and soft music playing in the background. Then suddenly you stand up and rush out. Over all that noise, you've heard your child crying—though no one else heard a thing. Those mama ears of yours can always hear when your little one needs you.

Just as a mother is tuned in to her child's cries, you can be in tune with the Holy Spirit. God doesn't always speak with grand plans and visible signs. Rather, He often uses the still, small voice of the Holy Spirit speaking through His Word. And it is only through practice and persistence that you'll be able to recognize it.

But just as a mother is always listening for her child's cries over the noise of a party or in the midst of the deepest sleep, as you spend more time with God, you'll find yourself always listening for the Holy Spirit's leadings. Turn your ear to the Lord, listen to Him speak, and find peace in His leading.

...................................................................

*Lord, help me to know Your voice intimately so I can hear You as You guide me each day. May I not miss even a whisper.*

*"Which of you by being anxious can add
a single hour to his span of life?"*
MATTHEW 6:27 ESV

*E*ach day has a tendency to fly by, leaving you out of breath and out of energy, and you're not sure how to change your situation. After all, a mom's work is never done! But have you ever considered structuring your week so it's more conducive to a balance of work and rest?

Make a schedule at the beginning of the week, and fill in all of your must-do items. As you list them, ask yourself if any of the items can be shared or altered. Can you figure out a carpool for your kid's after-school activities? Can you swap prepared meals with a friend or coworker? Can you better use the alone time you do have—during your commute, early in the morning or late at night, or on your lunch break? After seeing the structure of your week, you may be able to tweak it and allow yourself a time of rest every day.

Creating a balanced week won't simply fall into your waiting arms; it takes discipline and planning, but it will be worth it, both for you and your family.

...............................................................

*God, help me be discerning about my time so I can create more balance for my family's schedule. Help me bring order and rest to our lives this week.*

......................................................................

......................................................................

......................................................................

......................................................................

......................................................................

......................................................................

......................................................................

......................................................................

......................................................................

......................................................................

......................................................................

......................................................................

......................................................................

......................................................................

......................................................................

......................................................................

......................................................................

*In God I trust and am not afraid. What can man do to me?*
—PSALM 56:11

Life can be filled with many fears. Do you remember the fear you had as a child when you were learning to ride a bicycle? The only way you overcame that fear was to trust that your parent or another adult would not let you fall. Kneepads, training wheels, and a helmet helped too! Now, as a mom, you get to experience this exercise in trust from the perspective of a parent, knowing you always have your child's best interests in mind and you want to keep them safe.

The psalmist wrote about the awesome power of trust for those times when you are afraid. He knew and understood the power of God. The Bible has warned us that in this life we will suffer and experience difficulties (John 16:33). But you know what? It is during those times that you can activate your hope by placing your trust in God. Complete and total trust in God is the key to overcoming fear. When you trust God, giving in to fear is not an option. Trusting God means turning to Him in even the darkest times and trusting Him to make things right.

Are you fearful? Know that God is good, and He loves you and your kids. Conquer your fears by connecting with God through prayer. Then with hope-infused anticipation, look forward to what is coming.

..............................................................

*Father, You are worthy of my trust. Please empower me with Your strength and help me release my fears to You.*

*I pray that from his glorious, unlimited resources he will
empower you with inner strength through his Spirit.*

EPHESIANS 3:16 NLT

I magine yourself as you go through a day with one of your precious children. But instead of treating that child with love and gentleness, you place high demands on her. You wake her up after she's had only a few hours of sleep, you make her skip breakfast so she can scrub the floors, and you allow her to eat only as you're rushing out the door. After she finishes school for the day, you hand her an impossible to-do list—and when dinnertime comes and she hasn't completed it, you complain to her about it. You keep her up way past her bedtime and then make her feel guilty when she falls asleep on the couch.

This example may sound extreme. After all, who would treat a child that way? But isn't this the way you tend to treat yourself?

Self-care is so easy to neglect—especially as a single mom—but it's essential for living a healthy life. So today, try treating yourself like a child: relax your expectations, be kind to yourself, and rest when you get overwhelmed. Care for yourself as the precious child of God that you are.

.................................................................

*Lord, help me tend to my own physical, spiritual, and emotional needs and
care for myself as I take care of my children.*

*How long, O LORD? Will you forget me forever? How long will*
*you hide your face from me? . . . But I have trusted in your*
*steadfast love; my heart shall rejoice in your salvation. I will*
*sing to the LORD, because he has dealt bountifully with me.*

PSALM 13:1, 5–6 ESV

The psalmist David made lots of mistakes and suffered the consequences. He often felt far from God, and at times, he even despaired. But even when God felt far away from him, David knew he could trust in the Lord's unfailing love.

Are you going through a painful time in your life? You may be suffering physical pain, or perhaps you've lost a loved one. Maybe you are experiencing depression, maybe you feel a deep loneliness, or maybe the weight of solo parenting weighs heavily on you. There are many ways pain can appear in our lives, and it can feel like an impossible burden.

Take heart, dear mama: when life is painful, the Lord is right beside you. God isn't far away, up in the sky, ignoring you. Rather, He is bearing the pain right along with you. He is wrapping His arms around you and shedding tears with you. Cry out to Him, and find rest in His comfort and strength.

. . . . . . . . . . . . . . . . . . . . . . . . . . . . . . . . . . . . . . . . . . . . . . . . . . . . . . . .

*Father, some days this pain feels like too much for me to carry alone. Please*
*help me remember that You are always here to bear my burdens.*

*"The Lord make his face shine on you and be gracious to you;*
*the Lord turn his face toward you and give you peace."*

NUMBERS 6:25–26

We women can tend to be our own worst critics. When we make a mistake on a work project, yell at our kids, or put our foot in our mouth, we're often the ones beating ourselves up again and again and again. Moms, it's time we give ourselves a little grace.

Has mommy guilt, productivity guilt, or just plain life guilt reared its ugly head this week? Know that you don't need to keep replaying your mistakes or reliving your bad moments. God does not hold any resentment toward you. He sees you and all the responsibilities you are carrying as a single mom. You can breathe deeply knowing you are loved just as you are—flaws and all. You can find comfort in the Savior who washes you clean, over and over. So revel in the fact that you are covered with grace. And when you begin chastising yourself, when those words of self-condemnation ring in your ears, try to see yourself through the eyes of your loving Father.

Give yourself grace, even when you fall short or make a mistake. Rest in the knowledge that He removes all your sins from you gladly and willingly the moment that you ask.

................................................................

*Lord, teach me to give myself grace when I fall short and to embrace Your unconditional love and forgiveness.*

*⸙⸙⸙⸙⸙⸙* Day 7 *⸙⸙⸙⸙⸙⸙*

*"I am leaving you with a gift—peace of mind
and heart. And the peace I give is a gift the world
cannot give. So don't be troubled or afraid."*

John 14:27 NLT

When Jesus called for the tired and worn out to come to Him so He could give them peace, it can sound too good to be true for single moms. But He wasn't offering empty words. He didn't say it to be nice or to gain more followers; Jesus said He would give us peace because He knows it's what we need—as women and as parents—and the Lord always honors His Word.

If you worry that asking God for peace of mind and heart is burdensome or bothersome to Him, be encouraged, because just the opposite is true. He is waiting for you to come to Him; He wants you to ask Him for peace. He longs for all weary moms to be free from anxiety and fear and to enjoy life and their children to the fullest.

What a breath of encouragement! When the world cannot give us calm in the chaos, Jesus declared that He would. That is a promise. That is a declaration. He will give you peace—true peace—dear mama.

...........................................................................

*Jesus, please show this anxious mom how to truly find peace by releasing my burdens to You.*

........................................................................

........................................................................

........................................................................

........................................................................

........................................................................

........................................................................

........................................................................

........................................................................

........................................................................

........................................................................

........................................................................

........................................................................

........................................................................

........................................................................

........................................................................

........................................................................

........................................................................

........................................................................

........................................................................

........................................................................

*[Do] not giv[e] up meeting together, as some are in*
*the habit of doing, but encourag[e] one another—and*
*all the more as you see the Day approaching.*

HEBREWS 10:25

It's not easy to ask for help. Our culture prides itself on self-sufficiency. We look with envy at those women and moms who seem to "do it all." Asking for help may make us feel weak or embarrassed, and we don't want to burden others with our needs.

Asking for help requires vulnerability. It isn't easy, but ultimately it's an act of self-care. By taking a risk and being vulnerable, you encourage others to be vulnerable too. And wouldn't you like to have people around you who are open about their struggles rather than just putting on a brave face every day? It might be up to you to begin the movement.

Ask someone in your circle for help. It might be a best friend, a coworker, or a neighbor. You don't need to be ashamed. In fact, you'll likely find that you aren't alone in your struggles. Then when others need help, your example just may empower them to ask for the same.

...........................................................

*It's hard to ask for help, Lord, when it seems like other women and moms have it all together. Please give me the courage to be vulnerable with a few trusted people.*

......................................................................

......................................................................

......................................................................

......................................................................

......................................................................

......................................................................

......................................................................

......................................................................

......................................................................

......................................................................

......................................................................

......................................................................

......................................................................

......................................................................

......................................................................

......................................................................

......................................................................

......................................................................

*The fruit of the Spirit is love, joy, peace, patience, kindness,*
*goodness, faithfulness, gentleness, self-control.*

GALATIANS 5:22–23 ESV

Can you recite the fruit of the Spirit? You may know them—love, joy, peace, patience, kindness, goodness, faithfulness, gentleness, and self-control—but can you still exemplify them when you're exhausted and worn down? You may know them by heart, but do you hold them in your heart? Do you show gentleness and self-control when you're running on four hours of sleep? Are you able to be patient when you come home after working twelve hours straight and your children are fighting? Knowing the fruit of the Spirit is easy; living them is not.

When you are overwhelmed and overworked and you aren't making time to sit in God's presence, other attributes can rise, such as impatience, anger, jealousy, and selfishness. But when your body and mind are rested, and when you are immersing yourself in the words of God, the fruit of the Spirit spring forth much more easily.

Take a few quiet moments to read through the fruit of the Spirit, and ask God to help you better live these things out in your life.

*Fill me with Your presence, God, so that I can be a mom who lives out the fruit of the Spirit each day as an example to my children.*

..........................................................................................

..........................................................................................

..........................................................................................

..........................................................................................

..........................................................................................

..........................................................................................

..........................................................................................

..........................................................................................

..........................................................................................

..........................................................................................

..........................................................................................

..........................................................................................

..........................................................................................

..........................................................................................

..........................................................................................

..........................................................................................

..........................................................................................

..........................................................................................

..........................................................................................

..........................................................................................

*Make every effort to live in peace with everyone and to*
*be holy; without holiness no one will see the Lord.*

HEBREWS 12:14

We all have difficult relationships at some point in our lives. Whether it's with our parents, an ex-spouse, siblings, fellow churchgoers, coworkers, friends, or children, relational turmoil is unavoidable. We are broken people, and we sometimes say and do hurtful things to one another. We don't always get along with everyone. We let our egos and our traumas keep us from connecting with others as their authentic selves.

Is there a tumultuous relationship in your life? Is it giving you anxiety or keeping you up at night? Do you have a knot in your stomach when you think about that person? If so, tell the Lord about it. Ask Him to reveal truth to your heart.

Navigating broken relationships can be stressful, awkward, and painful. But when you are walking with the Lord, He can lift that burden from you and guide you along His perfect pathway. Ask Him to give you peace in this tough relationship today. And find divine freedom in knowing that He delights in walking alongside His children, even in the most difficult times.

............................................................................

*Father, You know the stress and anxiety this difficult relationship causes*
*me. Please strengthen me so I can do my best to be at peace with this person.*

........................................................................

........................................................................

........................................................................

........................................................................

........................................................................

........................................................................

........................................................................

........................................................................

........................................................................

........................................................................

........................................................................

........................................................................

........................................................................

........................................................................

........................................................................

........................................................................

........................................................................

........................................................................

*"You will seek me and find me when you
seek me with all your heart."*

JEREMIAH 29:13

A part of human nature is to have desires and seek something better for your future. It's also a huge part of motherhood: wanting to give your kids a better life than what you had. How you respond and seek solutions to the difficulties and problems that inevitably arise in life reveals how much optimism and perseverance you have.

Seeking something better is a common theme throughout the Scriptures. Pursuing God shows that you need Him and want what He has to offer. God told the prophet Jeremiah to tell the Israelites that if they sought Him with their whole hearts, He would be found.

This is essentially what Jesus told His disciples when He was teaching them to pray. He said, "Ask and it will be given to you; seek and you will find; knock and the door will be opened to you" (Matthew 7:7). Jesus knew that life would be difficult, so He wanted His disciples, and believers today, to persist in seeking God for help and for solutions.

When you cry out to the Lord, it conveys that you are seeking something better and looking for solutions. God moves your heart to pray because He wants to have a relationship with you.

.......................................................................

*Dear God, please help me to remain persistent in seeking You as I try to*
*better life for my children and myself.*

*Two are better than one, because they have a good return for*
*their labor: If either of them falls down, one can help the other*
*up. But pity anyone who falls and has no one to help them up.*

ECCLESIASTES 4:9–10

The best of friends make you feel at peace. You feel safe seeing them while dressed in your most casual clothes, inviting them over on your messiest house days, and entrusting them with your kiddos when you need an extra hand. All pretenses dissolve, and you can tell them anything.

Other friendships might be more difficult. You may feel that you constantly need to prove yourself, that you always need to put your best foot forward, or that you need to cover up any insecurities. Does this describe any of your friendships? If so, ask the Lord to heal these relationships and to bring more authentic friendships into your life.

As Proverbs 17:17 says, "A friend loves at all times." A friend loves you when you're a mess and when you confess your mistakes. A friend loves you through good times and hard. True friendships aren't always just warm and fuzzy, but a friend should bring more encouragement than stress to your life. Thank God today for your best friendships.

...............................................................

*Lord, please help me show appreciation to my true friends, and for those*
*times when my friendships are lacking, please bring new friends into my*
*life.*

........................................................................................

........................................................................................

........................................................................................

........................................................................................

........................................................................................

........................................................................................

........................................................................................

........................................................................................

........................................................................................

........................................................................................

........................................................................................

........................................................................................

........................................................................................

........................................................................................

........................................................................................

........................................................................................

........................................................................................

........................................................................................

........................................................................................

*The tongue has the power of life and death.*

PROVERBS 18:21

What words or phrases do you repeat over and over again? These may have been sayings a parent said to you when you were growing up or maybe phrases you say to your kids. Do these sayings that come to mind bring you comfort, laughter, spread hope or show love? Or do they cause you to feel discouraged?

People proliferate love or hate, encouragement or discouragement, through their words. James, the brother of Jesus, said words can cause a lot of damage that cannot be undone. James compared this damage to a fire that is out of control (James 3:6). It begins as a small flame that grows to engulf a forest; then it jumps from one hill to the next.

Measure your words before you speak by asking yourself if the words will cause pain. Words that hurt include lying, gossiping, putting someone down, cheating, and bragging, among others. Try adding a few encouraging words and phrases into your daily vocabulary, such as *awesome, amazing, way to go, thanks, I appreciate you,* and *I love you.* It only takes a word or two to lift someone's spirits, appreciate someone, or give a compliment. Then be ready for kind words to return to you.

...............................................................................

*Lord, thank You for words that encourage and bless me. May my words be encouraging and lift the spirits of my children and those around me.*

...................................................................................

...................................................................................

...................................................................................

...................................................................................

...................................................................................

...................................................................................

...................................................................................

...................................................................................

...................................................................................

...................................................................................

...................................................................................

...................................................................................

...................................................................................

...................................................................................

...................................................................................

...................................................................................

...................................................................................

...................................................................................

...................................................................................

*The LORD will fulfill his purpose for me.*
PSALM 138:8 ESV

God created the world. He made the mighty sun that warms the earth and the powerful oceans that cascade waves onto the shore, including all the creatures that inhabit the seas, both small and great. Everything that God has made has a purpose.

Take seashells, for example. Have you ever strolled along the beach with your child, with a sand bucket in hand, searching for seashells? When you would catch a glimmer of a seashell's color in the sparkling grains of sand, your little one would rush to scoop up this tiny treasure. Each beautifully designed shell once served as a home for a little sea creature. Though the sea creature has moved on, the empty shell, having fulfilled its purpose, is left behind. It is a small reminder of God as Creator and His purpose fulfilled.

As single moms carrying *so* much each day, it's easy to become consumed by busyness. Even good things can become distractions that take our eyes away from our great God, who created each of us for a purpose, just as He created the tiny seashells. Everything God has made has a purpose, which He will fulfill in His time. Rest in this amazing truth, and allow it to give you hope.

.........................................................................

*Heavenly Father, thank You for creating my kids and me with unique purposes. I will rest in the hope that You will fulfill each purpose in Your time.*

........................................................................

........................................................................

........................................................................

........................................................................

........................................................................

........................................................................

........................................................................

........................................................................

........................................................................

........................................................................

........................................................................

........................................................................

........................................................................

........................................................................

........................................................................

........................................................................

........................................................................

........................................................................

........................................................................

*What is the best thing to do in the short life God has given us? I think we should enjoy eating, drinking, and working hard. This is what God intends for us to do.*

ECCLESIASTES 5:18 CEV

A strong work ethic is a great quality to have. You also want your kids to be hard workers—trying their best at school, completing their chores, and being committed team members if they participate in extracurricular activities. But sometimes a strong work ethic can actually work against you, such as when you begin working night and day, skipping meals, or getting too little sleep because you want to do your job well.

God calls us to work hard. He wants us to work to the best of our abilities and to honor and glorify Him through our efforts. But He doesn't want to see us burned out, struggling to stay healthy, becoming resentful of our jobs, and having nothing left at the end of the day to offer our children, family, and friends.

Does your work ethic work against you? Admit that you can't do it all—because you weren't created to do it all. Then treat yourself to some rest. Take a Sabbath; enjoy a weekend staycation. God worked hard, and then He rested. Take some time to follow His example.

..................................................................................

*Heavenly Father, remind me that You didn't create me to do it all and that I need to follow Your example and rest.*

*My God will meet all your needs according to
the riches of his glory in Christ Jesus.*
PHILIPPIANS 4:19

You ou swipe your credit card to pay for groceries and inwardly wince. You put your tithe in the offering plate at church and pray the Lord will provide. You're an expert with coupons. You try to pick up odd jobs here and there, and maybe you even work multiple jobs regularly. Still, more often than not, there's more month at the end of your money.

If you're wrestling with financial worries as a single mom, hear these words: God knows your needs. He knows how much those car repairs will cost, when the next school fee is due, and how much those braces will cost in the future. He's intimately involved in your life, and He cares deeply about you and your well-being.

Take a deep breath and feel the air rush through your lungs. The Lord—who formed your airways and the very oxygen molecules that fill them—knows everything you need, and He promises to provide for you and your family. Cling to His promises today. When your finances look bleak, rest in the provision of the cross.

......................................................................

*You promise to provide for me, Lord. When I am anxious about money,
please help me to trust Your words.*

*We are God's handiwork, created in Christ Jesus to do good*
*works, which God prepared in advance for us to do.*

EPHESIANS 2:10

You are an accountant, nurse, teacher, musician. You are a mother, sister, aunt, friend. You are gentle and loyal, feisty and funny, intelligent and strong. You are adventurous, thoughtful, energetic, and wholly unique. You are so many things wrapped into one body.

You are a delight. But you may not feel delightful; you may feel weak, discouraged, overwhelmed, or angry. You might even wish you were a completely different person. But guess what? You're you, and there's no one else like you. You're individually made with unique gifts. Your mind, voice, laugh, and personality are wonderfully irreplaceable.

Do you truly know yourself? Spend some time thinking about what makes you who you are. Connect with your authentic self. Stop trying to be the woman and mom that you're not—and start being the person God created you to be: yourself. Rest in that thought today, and every time you begin to criticize yourself, ask your Maker for perspective. Embrace yourself, and find rest in who you are—a beloved child of God.

.......................................................................................

*Heavenly Father, when I am tempted to be someone I'm not, remind me that I'm Your beloved child and You delight in me.*

........................................................................

........................................................................

........................................................................

........................................................................

........................................................................

........................................................................

........................................................................

........................................................................

........................................................................

........................................................................

........................................................................

........................................................................

........................................................................

........................................................................

........................................................................

........................................................................

........................................................................

........................................................................

........................................................................

........................................................................

*Very early the next morning before daylight, Jesus got up*
*and went to a place where he could be alone and pray.*

MARK 1:35 CEV

If you were to commit an entire day to simply resting, would you feel guilty? Many moms would. But resting shouldn't go hand in hand with guilt. Give yourself permission to rest and enjoy it. Resting will make you a healthier, happier, and more relaxed woman and mom.

If you feel guilty about resting, remember that Jesus rested. He rested so that He could minister to others more effectively, and He invited His disciples to rest with Him. Even though He knew His time on earth was finite and He had so much to accomplish, He drew away from the crowds and made sure His human body was replenished. Rest is essential for your spiritual, emotional, and physical well-being; it should not cause you to feel guilty.

What are some ways that you can create pockets of rest within your day today? Can you take a few moments to breathe deeply and quiet your mind instead of checking your phone? Can you get to bed a few minutes earlier tonight, knowing that some things can wait till tomorrow? Plan times of rest this week, and enjoy them. Rest is a gift from God!

*Lord, I feel guilty when I try to rest. Help me remember that rest is a gift from You.*

*What do people get for all the toil and anxious*
*striving with which they labor under the sun?*
ECCLESIASTES 2:22

Social media can be fun, but it also can be a harmful distraction that wrecks your self-esteem and contentment. If you find yourself trying to compare your life to what you see online, you're going to be disappointed, dear mama. These images and videos are only snapshots and sound bites of another's life. They may truly be representative of only one minute out of someone's day or week.

If you feel the pressure to make your life look picture-perfect, try taking a break from social media. Instead of experiencing your life and kids through the lens of a phone camera, put down your phone and be present in the moment. Life may be messy, broken, tear-stained, and tough. But there are also those moments that make you laugh out loud and shout with joy, holy moments that will remain engrained in your mind forever. It's your life, your family, and your home—in all their glorious imperfection.

Life doesn't need to be photo-worthy to be worth a great deal. Step away from the pressure of a living a picture-perfect life. You'll be glad you did.

.......................................................................

*Remind me, Jesus, that this life really is about loving and pleasing You and*
*raising little ones who will follow You.*

*"Are you tired? Worn out? . . . Come to me. Get away with me and you'll recover your life. I'll show you how to take a real rest."*

MATTHEW 11:28 MSG

A re you weary, discouraged, stressed, or afraid? Does the busyness of your week ahead make you angry instead of excited? Do you have a big deadline coming up at work or an extended family event you're nervous about? Bring your burdens to the Lord. He wants all of your mess and all of your stress—your exhaustion, pain, frustration, and sin. He wants to hear you call His name and ask Him for help—and He will be quick to rescue you.

Don't let one more moment come between you and the One who gave His life for you. Call on His name, and ask Him to relieve you of your burdens. In Scripture, Jesus clearly stated that He wants to give His people rest—not just for a minute or an hour; He wants to give us complete and unending rest.

Jesus didn't say, "Come to Me when you have everything figured out." He simply said, "Come to Me." Call out His name, and let Him take your burdens away and replace them with His love, joy, peace, and rest.

*I can't do this on my own anymore, Lord, and I'm asking You for help. Rescue me with Your rest.*

........................................................................

........................................................................

........................................................................

........................................................................

........................................................................

........................................................................

........................................................................

........................................................................

........................................................................

........................................................................

........................................................................

........................................................................

........................................................................

........................................................................

........................................................................

........................................................................

........................................................................

*Bear with each other and forgive one another if any of you has a*
*grievance against someone. Forgive as the Lord forgave you.*

COLOSSIANS 3:13

When others mistreat you, complaining may feel good at first, but later, it often will leave you feeling even more frustrated than before. Instead of complaining, consider giving grace.

If someone offends you, do you have the grace and courage to turn the other cheek? When a coworker annoys you or your co-parent ticks you off, do you seek a solution—or look for someone to rant to? Yes, there are times when you need to confront people, speak truth into others' lives, or gently educate them on their wrongdoings. It's good to be assertive and stand up for yourself and advocate for your children's best interests. But other times, you simply need to give grace.

The next time you feel your temper rise or your frustration level increase, ask yourself if this is really an opportunity to offer grace. Maybe you just need to walk away, take a deep breath, and pray for guidance. God gives us grace upon grace, and when you offer it to others, you can experience a peace that passes understanding.

..................................................................

*Lord, when I get frustrated with others, give me discernment about when I*
*need to speak up for myself and my family and when I need to simply offer*
*grace.*

..............................................................................

..............................................................................

..............................................................................

..............................................................................

..............................................................................

..............................................................................

..............................................................................

..............................................................................

..............................................................................

..............................................................................

..............................................................................

..............................................................................

..............................................................................

..............................................................................

..............................................................................

..............................................................................

..............................................................................

..............................................................................

*Give thanks in all circumstances; for this is*
*God's will for you in Christ Jesus.*

I Thessalonians 5:18

As a mom, you began teaching your kids manners at an early age. Before your child could speak, you may have even taught the sign language signs for *please* and *thank you*.

There is power in being thankful and appreciating what you have. You can turn your problems into joys when you view them as opportunities to change your circumstances. Paul taught that in connection with everything we go through in life, we are to face it with gratitude. Thankfulness is the first step to opening up your mind and heart to replace hurt with hope. Thankfulness means there is a recognition that God is in control.

Gratitude is the art of using your faith to seek and discover the blessings within problems and in routine, ordinary tasks in life. Thankfulness evolves from a heart of hope and joy as you dwell on God's mercy and His work on your behalf. Take time today to think of a way that God has blessed you. Acknowledge God's goodness and thank Him for His many blessings.

...............................................................................

*Dear God, thank You for the blessing of Your work in my life and in my children's lives. I choose to rejoice that You are working out everything in life for our good and Your glory.*

........................................................................................

........................................................................................

........................................................................................

........................................................................................

........................................................................................

........................................................................................

........................................................................................

........................................................................................

........................................................................................

........................................................................................

........................................................................................

........................................................................................

........................................................................................

........................................................................................

........................................................................................

........................................................................................

........................................................................................

........................................................................................

........................................................................................

*We know that God causes everything to work*
*together for the good of those who love God and are*
*called according to his purpose for them.*

ROMANS 8:28 NLT

D o you ever feel like you have run out of options? You have tried everything you can think of to find a new job, get a promotion, or simply figure out a new direction that will lead to a better life for you and your kids. You have listened to trusted friends and family, read books, but nothing seems to open a new door. Could you really be out of possibilities?

Of course not! God may be using these situations as opportunities for growth to instruct you or move you to a different place. Every difficulty has a purpose when you are a child of God and are seeking His direction for your life. You may see your waiting period as a waste, but God sees it as an opportunity to create a change in your life. His direction and design may not be what you expected or happen as quickly as you hoped, but He will use your faith to make something more wonderful than you could have ever imagined. You can trust in the Designer of all your hopes and your possibilities.

....................................................................................

*Dear God, sometimes things do not work out in ways that I expected or as quickly as I had hoped. Thank You that You can make even my worst days work for my good.*

*You will keep in perfect peace those whose minds*
*are steadfast, because they trust in you.*

ISAIAH 26:3

Your body and mind cry, *Go to bed*, but you refuse because there are still half a dozen things to finish up for the day. Sound familiar? While some tasks must be finished (a work project, feeding the baby, paying a bill), there are many other responsibilities that can be put off for another time.

If you feel exhausted, ask yourself, *Are there negative consequences for not finishing this today?* Then weigh the pros and cons. Sometimes you have to push through and finish up. But often, it's simply pride or stubbornness that stands between you and rest. It's easy to feel that everything's urgent and that it all falls on your shoulders. If you don't do it, who will? And if you don't do it now, won't it be just another thing to add to tomorrow's already full to-do list?

But even if things aren't finished, if the house is a mess and the dishes are piled in the sink, even if you aren't finished packing or the room is half-painted, rest is more important. Let yourself off the hook, and allow yourself to rest even if a few things must remain undone.

.......................................................................

*God, I want to make rest my priority when it's what I truly need most. Help me trust that everything else will fall into place.*

*After his suffering, [Jesus] presented himself to them and gave many convincing proofs that he was alive. He appeared to them over a period of forty days and spoke about the kingdom of God.*

ACTS 1:3

If you watch the news for five minutes, listen to talk radio, or scan an online news site, you'll know our world is broken. Violence, war, injustice, racism, poverty, and more seem to be running rampant—and some days it seems the world is just getting worse and worse. The headlines are enough to make you want to hug your children tighter and consider never letting them leave the house again. Maybe the headlines even make you feel like *you* never want to leave the house again.

Take heart; when the world feels brutal and overwhelmingly broken, God is still working. When the headlines cut through your soul and the most recent news makes your breath catch, you can find courage because God's love and redemption will prevail in the end.

Today our world is full of suffering. But suffering doesn't get the last word. The almighty God gets the last word—and He promises rest, restoration, and healing. Cling to that knowledge today, and rest in the enduring promises of a very big, very powerful, very loving God.

........................................................................

*Lord, when the world feels absolutely brutal and broken, may I see glimpses of Your love and grace.*

......................................................................................

......................................................................................

......................................................................................

......................................................................................

......................................................................................

......................................................................................

......................................................................................

......................................................................................

......................................................................................

......................................................................................

......................................................................................

......................................................................................

......................................................................................

......................................................................................

......................................................................................

......................................................................................

......................................................................................

......................................................................................

......................................................................................

*Who compares with you among gods, O GOD? Who
compares with you in power, in holy majesty, in
awesome praises, wonder-working God?*

EXODUS 15:11 MSG

C hildren are the best at enjoying the small things—a solitary
bubble, a caterpillar, a balloon, a ride on the lawn mower, a dan-
delion. It doesn't matter if it's a tiny puddle or a huge swimming pool,
a trip to the mall or to Disney World; kids are able to see even the smallest of moments and things as opportunities for wonder and joy.

When did we lose that childlike amazement? When did we become
so hard to impress and so difficult to captivate? With all the responsibilities of single motherhood, it can feel like there's no time to "stop and
smell the roses." It can feel like we're always in survival mode. That's
why many days we rush past so many tiny but great moments—simply
because we're too busy or too distracted, trying to keep things together
and just make it through the day.

Give yourself permission to slow down today. Let your gaze linger
over the sunrise, savor a delicious meal while engaging all your senses,
and be on the lookout for the amazing and beautiful. God has placed it
all around you. Open your eyes, and take in its wonder.

.................................................................

*Heavenly Father, give me the eyes of a child today. Please help me slow
down, refocus, and be on the lookout for Your wonders all around me.*

..................................................................................................

..................................................................................................

..................................................................................................

..................................................................................................

..................................................................................................

..................................................................................................

..................................................................................................

..................................................................................................

..................................................................................................

..................................................................................................

..................................................................................................

..................................................................................................

..................................................................................................

..................................................................................................

..................................................................................................

..................................................................................................

..................................................................................................

..................................................................................................

*The righteous person may have many troubles,*
*but the Lord delivers him from them all.*
Psalm 34:19

When written in Chinese, the word *crisis* is composed of two characters—one represents *danger* and one represents *opportunity*. Along with danger, crisis is represented by opportunity. Ancient Chinese people used brush strokes that painted words with deeper meanings. Known for its beauty, grace, and history, the technique for this type of writing dates back to approximately four thousand years ago. Using this technique, the word *crisis* combines images of danger and opportunity.

No one is exempt from hardship. When you face dangers, disappointments, or losses, God can still bring about good from your circumstances. When you overcome problems and learn new perspectives, you will find the hope of new opportunities. That hope comes from the knowledge that God will help you in a time of trouble and He promises to deliver you.

Let a crisis bring out the best in you. It allows you to become courageous and an overcomer. As you focus on solutions, with help from God, you will discover you are stronger than you thought.

.................................................................................

*Dear God, thank You for new opportunities that are born in a crisis. Allow me to face them courageously because You are with me.*

........................................................................

........................................................................

........................................................................

........................................................................

........................................................................

........................................................................

........................................................................

........................................................................

........................................................................

........................................................................

........................................................................

........................................................................

........................................................................

........................................................................

........................................................................

........................................................................

........................................................................

........................................................................

........................................................................

........................................................................

........................................................................

*Out of his fullness we have all received grace*
*in place of grace already given.*

John 1:16

You messed up. You lost your temper. You crossed the line. You chose evil over good. You hurt someone you love. Do any of these statements ring true in your life today?

As humans, women, and moms, we fall over and over again. We shake our heads at our mistakes, feel shame, beat ourselves up, and disappoint many. We fall into temptation's trap, act unjustly, and let sin rule our minds. But still, there is grace—grace upon grace upon grace—and the very real assurance of God's never-ending grace is like a deep well of water for a thirsty soul.

God knows we are sinners. He knows our shortcomings and struggles. He knows about that sin we can't seem to break free from, and He offers us grace. It doesn't make sense, and it isn't contingent on anything we do; instead, it's a reflection of God's goodness and mercy.

Dear friend, rest assured: there is grace enough for you. All you have to do is ask for it, and God will cover you with His forgiveness and love.

...................................................................

*I don't deserve Your grace, yet You lavish it upon me over and over again. Thank You, Lord.*

......................................................................

......................................................................

......................................................................

......................................................................

......................................................................

......................................................................

......................................................................

......................................................................

......................................................................

......................................................................

......................................................................

......................................................................

......................................................................

......................................................................

......................................................................

......................................................................

......................................................................

......................................................................

......................................................................

......................................................................

*Let your face shine on your servant; save*
*me in your unfailing love.*

PSALM 31:16

B ecause rest is important for our spiritual growth, Satan will do everything he can to keep us busy and distracted. One of the most common ways he ensures we don't rest is through guilt. Do you ever feel guilty if you take time to rest? Do you feel as if you're failing as a person? As a mother? Maybe you believe on some level that your worth is found in your productivity. When you feel this way, think of the example set for us by our Creator.

God worked for six days. He formed tall, sturdy oaks; poured light into fireflies; and made people in His own image—and then, He rested. Without guilt and without shame. The Lord worked, and then He rested. The Lord did it as an example for His children.

When we rest, we aren't neglecting our duties, and we aren't being lazy. But we are giving our souls a chance to breathe and redirecting our minds to thoughts of the Lord. Rest benefits our physical bodies and our spiritual beings. It should be met with thanksgiving, not guilt. Give thanks that the Lord knew we needed rest, and so He created it at the beginning of time.

*Take away my shame and guilt, dear Jesus, and help me enjoy the blessing of rest.*

........................................................

........................................................

........................................................

........................................................

........................................................

........................................................

........................................................

........................................................

........................................................

........................................................

........................................................

........................................................

........................................................

........................................................

........................................................

........................................................

........................................................

........................................................

*I would have lain down and been quiet; I would*
*have slept; then I would have been at rest.*

JOB 3:13 ESV

When a plant is thriving, it grows healthy and strong, producing flowers, fruit, or vegetables. When a baby is thriving, they are gaining weight, becoming aware of surroundings, and hitting developmental milestones. But what does it look like for you to thrive?

Understand that God wants you to thrive and to live life abundantly. Sometimes thriving looks like adventure and spontaneity, while at other times thriving means quiet, stillness, and rest. If you're in a particularly busy season of life and motherhood, thriving may simply mean having a clear mind and content spirit.

Instead of striving this week, ask God how He wants you to thrive. And remember that thriving doesn't always mean producing; sometimes it means lounging in an easy chair with a book, taking a leisurely walk around the neighborhood with your children, or simply sitting and watching the sunset with your Savior.

How can you thrive today? Take a moment to let God show you where you need nurturing so that you can focus on creating space where you can better flourish.

...................................................................

*You know what's best for me, Lord. Please teach me to thrive instead of*
*strive in my life and parenting.*

........................................................................................

........................................................................................

........................................................................................

........................................................................................

........................................................................................

........................................................................................

........................................................................................

........................................................................................

........................................................................................

........................................................................................

........................................................................................

........................................................................................

........................................................................................

........................................................................................

........................................................................................

........................................................................................

........................................................................................

........................................................................................

........................................................................................

........................................................................................

*When Jesus heard what had happened, he withdrew*
*by boat privately to a solitary place.*

MATTHEW 14:13

S ome people believe that the only suffering Jesus experienced was His passion during the week of His crucifixion and death on the cross. But according to Scripture, Jesus suffered and grieved several times in His life. On one occasion Jesus was grieved at the loss of His cousin, John the Baptist. Herod had thrown John in prison. Then Herod's wife tricked Herod into ordering the beheading of John. She was angry at John for condemning the couple for living together. When Jesus heard about John's death, He withdrew to a solitary place.

Disasters, loss, and crises help you understand the pain and adversity that all people will experience at one time or another. Once you have suffered, you have empathy for others and can provide comfort to someone else. Through the death of John, Jesus understood what it meant to suffer the loss of a loved one.

If you're going through a tough time and could use support from like-minded individuals, it may be helpful for you to find a support group through a local church, ministry, or counseling center. This may be just what you need to help you renew your hope.

*Dear God, thank You that others understand my losses because of their experiences. Thank You for the compassion we share.*

························································································

························································································

························································································

························································································

························································································

························································································

························································································

························································································

························································································

························································································

························································································

························································································

························································································

························································································

························································································

························································································

························································································

························································································

························································································

*"My sheep listen to my voice; I know them, and they follow me."*

JOHN 10:27

Have you ever stopped yourself from dreaming because your aspirations didn't seem practical as a single mom, as if they were too far out of your reach? Have you been afraid to hope because you thought something bad would happen? If so, you may need to reframe your thoughts.

God reveals His will for you in several different ways: through His Word; through His still, small voice; through your circumstances; and through other people. Many times He may be using any one of these ways to communicate an action that He wants you to do or a new path you should take. But you must learn to listen so you can know what God wants you to do.

Learn to recognize God's voice so you can hear when the Holy Spirit speaks to you. He may be guiding you to renew your dreams—or simply keep your dream alive. Then take whatever small steps you can at this time to obey His leading. Close your eyes and remember what made your goal so special. Free your thoughts from negativity, and follow God's leading to hope and dream even bigger than before.

...............................................................................

*Lord, please help me to know and recognize Your voice so I can follow as You lead me. Please help me to hold on with hope to the dreams You have for my life.*

......................................................................

......................................................................

......................................................................

......................................................................

......................................................................

......................................................................

......................................................................

......................................................................

......................................................................

......................................................................

......................................................................

......................................................................

......................................................................

......................................................................

......................................................................

......................................................................

......................................................................

*Jesus said, "Let's go off by ourselves to a quiet place and rest awhile." He said this because there were so many people coming and going that Jesus and his apostles didn't even have time to eat.*

MARK 6:31 NLT

When you're exhausted, everything is hard. Being patient with your kids and others is hard; excelling at work is hard. Bone-deep weariness can leave you feeling drained and dejected.

The Lord knows that your energy is spent and that the thought of living with this kind of continuous exhaustion makes you want to weep. Have you ever been so busy that you didn't have time to eat? Jesus experienced that in Mark 6:31. Ever feel like you live in your car, shuttling kids to school and other activities? Jesus got worn out traveling in John 4. Ever been so exhausted that you slept through your alarm? Jesus slept through a "furious storm" in Matthew 8:24. In His humanity, He needed to rest and recharge.

If you're feeling deeply weary today, ask for help. You don't have to do it all, and the truth is, you can't do it all. Call your closest friend and ask for help. Ask a church member or family member; tell your boss or your teammate that you need a break. When you're weary, don't force yourself to keep going in hopes that you'll find rest eventually. Find rest now. Ask for help.

.....................................................................................

*Lord, I am utterly exhausted. Please send people my way to help me find rest.*

........................................................................................

........................................................................................

........................................................................................

........................................................................................

........................................................................................

........................................................................................

........................................................................................

........................................................................................

........................................................................................

........................................................................................

........................................................................................

........................................................................................

........................................................................................

........................................................................................

........................................................................................

........................................................................................

........................................................................................

........................................................................................

........................................................................................

*Since we are surrounded by such a great cloud of witnesses, let us throw off everything that hinders and the sin that so easily entangles. And let us run with perseverance the race marked out for us.*

HEBREWS 12:1

You wanted to finish that big project at work, vacuum your home, take the car to the shop, check in with your parents, and quiz your child on their multiplication facts. But none of those things happened today, and you're left feeling really discouraged. We've all had those sorts of days.

Sometimes you may need to adjust your expectations. They may simply be too high, and you run the risk of getting stuck in a vicious cycle of unmet expectations. It's okay, at times, to throw up your hands and say, "I'll try again tomorrow." We can't do it all.

Is it time to ease up on your expectations a little? Would it really be disastrous if you didn't finish everything today? God promises to always take care of you—and that promise doesn't end if your to-do list isn't finished. After all, as long as we're breathing, there will always be something else that needs done. Let go of your expectations today, and instead, ask God to help you look at your day through the lens of His expectations.

...................................................................

*God, help me adjust my expectations and live according to Your plans, not my own.*

*I am certain that God, who began the good work*
*within you, will continue his work until it is finally*
*finished on the day when Christ Jesus returns.*

PHILIPPIANS 1:6 NLT

ope is a good and necessary thing. Looking forward with anticipation helps get us through long days. Kids love to count down
to Christmas or their birthdays. Adults may keep track of the weeks
until vacation. Some frazzled moms may calculate the number of days
until the kids go back to school. The days are hard, but good things
are coming! Yet life has a tendency to threaten to squash our hopes and
sink our expectations. Maybe you thought you'd have more financial
security, or perhaps you hoped you would have a different job. Is this
a time of disappointment or a time when your dreams are coming true?

Whether your days are filled with hopeful excitement, dashed
dreams, or somewhere in between, take comfort in this fact: God
knows where you came from, and He knows where you are going.
He knows your past and your future; He knows your every hope and
dream. Rather than hoping for and expecting great things of your life,
why not hope for and expect great things of your great God? You can
trust the certainty that He will never disappoint you.

...........................................................................

*Thank You for always coming through, Father, even when Your plans don't*
*match up with my own.*

..................................................................

..................................................................

..................................................................

..................................................................

..................................................................

..................................................................

..................................................................

..................................................................

..................................................................

..................................................................

..................................................................

..................................................................

..................................................................

..................................................................

..................................................................

..................................................................

..................................................................

..................................................................

..................................................................

..................................................................

..................................................................

# Day 36

*My heart is not proud, Lord, my eyes are not haughty;*
*I do not concern myself with great matters or things too*
*wonderful for me. But I have calmed and quieted myself.*

PSALM 131:1–2

Have you ever noticed that when you're worried or stressed, your breathing becomes different? Your breaths are small and shallow instead of deep and even, and you engage your shoulders instead of your diaphragm. Your jaw clenches and tightens. Because your lungs aren't fully filling with oxygen, you become short of breath, making you feel even more anxious.

You may not have time or money for a massage or a spa day right now, but you want to practice self-care. You want your body and mind to feel at rest. That's where inhaling, exhaling, and releasing come in.

If your breathing is shallow, take several deep breaths in a row. Let your breath expand your lungs and move your diaphragm. As you exhale, do so slowly and in a controlled manner. If your jaw is tense, move it back and forth and do some stretches with it; you may feel a little silly, but you will also feel better. Throughout the day, do this breathing and jaw check. If you feel tension, then inhale, exhale, release . . . and rest in your breathing.

*Lord, remind me to inhale, exhale, and release whenever I feel anxious.*

*For to us a child is born, to us a son is given, and the government*
*will be on his shoulders. And he will be called Wonderful*
*Counselor, Mighty God, Everlasting Father, Prince of Peace.*

ISAIAH 9:6

You think about last night, and you shake your head. There was so much you wanted to get done, but instead you fell asleep on the couch, completely exhausted. Your long to-do list just got longer.

Especially as a single mom, it can feel like everything falls on you. You're providing for your children in so many ways, building a home for them where they feel safe and loved—and that takes work. But don't forget that you need to care for yourself too.

Friend, be gentle with yourself. If you are weary, you need to rest. If you're falling behind in life's demands, you may be expecting too much of yourself. Be gentle, exceedingly gentle, with your tired body and mind.

When Jesus called the weary and heavy laden to Himself, He didn't berate or lecture them. Instead, He welcomed them, and He promised to carry their load (Matthew 11:28 NKJV). Why not give the Savior your heavy burdens? Hear His words of love and grace instead of your own words of negativity and condemnation. Find rest in the Prince of Peace.

..................................................................

*Dear loving Savior, please take this heavy load and fill me with peaceful rest.*

*May our Lord Jesus Christ himself and God our
Father . . . encourage your hearts and strengthen
you in every good deed and word.*

2 Thessalonians 2:16–17

When the sun sets and you fall into bed after a particularly rough day, do you ever feel as if the whole world is against you? Your kids are demanding, your work is stressing you out, your responsibilities are overwhelming, and everything would be so much better if you just had a little more time. Sound familiar?

Rest assured that after every bad night there is a new sunrise, every frustrating day can be followed by a joyful evening, and each bad start can end with a fantastic finish. Until the day is over, there's always the chance that it can turn around. And even when a day feels irredeemable, there's the hope of a fresh start the next day. Sometimes we just need to rest and start again tomorrow.

When God said His mercies are new every morning (Lamentations 3:22–23 NKJV), He meant it. He has more than enough grace for you each day. You can be sure of it—as sure as the sun rises. Find peace today knowing that God gives you new beginnings . . . over and over and over again.

.........................................................................

*Thank You, Jesus, for Your grace upon grace—every morning, evening,
and moment in between.*

*GOD told Samuel, "Looks aren't everything. . . .GOD
judges persons differently than humans do. Men and
women look at the face; GOD looks into the heart."*

I SAMUEL 16:7 MSG

In these days of oversharing via social media, does it feel like you're
constantly trying to impress people with your job, home, mothering,
or other aspects of your life? We want to present the best versions of
ourselves and hide the parts that make us feel less-than. We might crop
the unfolded laundry out of a photo or post an upbeat life update when
we're really feeling frustrated or lonely.

It's not doing you—or anyone else—any good. And, chances are,
you're more than a little tired. It's time to give trusted individuals a
key to the door of your real life. Letting others into the messy, raw,
frustrating, and joyful parts of your life is the most authentic thing you
can do. And authenticity brings freedom. It bypasses the superficial and
allows friendships to grow and respect to deepen. Being honest about
both the good and bad in life loosens your hold on that oh-so-phony
image.

Are you keeping others locked outside of your real life? Take a
chance and let them in. You'll be amazed by your ability to share more
easily and to find peace.

..............................................................................

*God, forgive me for wanting others to think I have it all together. Help me
instead to be open and honest with a few trusted people.*

*Teach us to number our days, that we may gain a heart of wisdom.*

PSALM 90:12

Moms are familiar with the saying, "The days are long, but the years are short." How often do you think about the next hour, day, month, or year? How often have you thought, *I can't wait until . . . ?* Do you find yourself wishing today would hurry up and be over so that you can get to what's next? If you find yourself rushing through the days, try to remember: this present day is God's gift to you.

In this present moment, God gives you breath. He keeps your heart beating. He woke you up this morning, and He reveals Himself to you throughout the day—through your child's laughter, the kindness of a stranger, the pink and orange hues of a sunset. You can never get this day back. You can never relive this age and stage of your child's life—or your own. Today is a gift for you to relish and enjoy fully.

Don't be so focused on the future that you miss the present; it is filled with God's blessings and gifts. There is much to be enjoyed in this day. Look for it, and then rest in the joy of this present moment.

......................................................................

*Jesus, when I'm wishing time would pass by more quickly, remind me that today is a gift from You.*

...........................................................................

...........................................................................

...........................................................................

...........................................................................

...........................................................................

...........................................................................

...........................................................................

...........................................................................

...........................................................................

...........................................................................

...........................................................................

...........................................................................

...........................................................................

...........................................................................

...........................................................................

...........................................................................

...........................................................................

...........................................................................

*"Mary has chosen what is better, and it*
*will not be taken away from her."*

LUKE 10:42

I *do not have time for that,* we say to ourselves. Busyness fills your schedule and can keep you from living with intention. The items on your calendar reflect your choices. With each choice you make, you control the hours before they arrive. The question is, does God like your busyness and the choices on your schedule?

The story of Mary and Martha in the book of Luke helps us to reflect on our priorities. These sisters who were friends of Jesus had welcomed Him into their home. Martha busied herself with the chores of the house, including preparing a meal, while Mary relaxed at the feet of Jesus. Many times we are like Martha with many tasks and activities vying for our time at our jobs, churches, and with our kids. The to-do list can be unending and fill our schedules so that time for God seems impossible to find.

If you want time for something, you need to evaluate how you are spending your weeks and hours. Decide if you need to let something go. Make God your priority, and then allocate time for everything else in your life.

.........................................................................

*Lord, instead of choosing to do what is good, help me learn to discern what is best. Today I choose to sit at Your feet.*

## Day 42

*Listen to my voice in the morning, LORD. Each morning*
*I bring my requests to you and wait expectantly.*

PSALM 5:3 NLT

When you pray, you expect God to listen and respond. Your hope is that He will answer your prayer in the way you have in mind. However, He knows what you need and will wisely provide what you need each day. Therefore, when you pray, you should wait. When you make the decision to wait on God, you may find some impatience that floats to the top because He does not respond according to our timing. However, in waiting, your eyes will be opened to His sovereign will, and you will learn that the sooner you trust His will, the sooner your expectations will be realized.

Waiting on God takes patience that is intertwined with hope. It teaches you that you can depend on Him to work on your behalf. You can afford to wait on God because only by His power are your prayers answered. After you pray, begin looking for His response. This is what the psalmist called "wait[ing] expectantly" (Psalm 5:3 NLT). God always answers prayer. God knows the future, and His future contains the best for you. He loves you and knows the right time to bless you with an answer. Trust that the wait will be worth it.

......................................................................

*God, I trust that You will bless me with an answer to my prayers. And if the*
*answer does not come right away, I will wait expectantly for Your response.*

*I am a friend to all who fear you, to all who follow your precepts.*

PSALM 119:63

There is nothing like a close companion who encourages you. You can trust that person and turn to them for support. If you feel like you are drowning, your companion will throw you a lifeline to pull you back up and encourage you to keep going.

But what if that friend were also a follower of Jesus, and what if there were millions of friends like that? Indeed, there are millions of people around the world who love the Lord. A relationship with God makes our friendships with one another have a closeness that is very special. There is a spiritual connection with one another and with God so that you should never feel alone or without support.

Share your hopes with a friend, and together seek to grow in your faith. You can laugh together at what goes wrong and rejoice together at what goes right. You will find your friend investing in you and your welfare. You can discuss your struggles and problems to get ideas from a different perspective. But more than that, you will have the wisdom and love of God and the support of others like you because of your common focus as believers.

........................................................................

*Dear God, thank You for the support of friends who love You the way that I do.*

*Whether you turn to the right or to the left, your ears will hear*
*a voice behind you, saying, "This is the way; walk in it."*

ISAIAH 30:21

I t's always a good feeling to fall into bed at the end of the day with
your to-do list neatly checked off, the laundry folded and put away,
and the kids' lunches packed and ready to go for tomorrow. Finishing
the list feels good. And it's good to focus and work hard, but not if
you're obsessed with "the list."

If you're basing the quality of your day on the number of items
checked off your list, that's not truly living. Take an occasional break
from the list. Leave the toys on the floor for tonight. Skip making
the bed. Leave work five minutes early to spend five extra minutes at
home. It might feel counterintuitive, but good things are often born
from going against the grain.

Remind yourself that life isn't about a list. God won't be shaking
His head at you if your day only consists of loving your kids and those
around you well. In fact, that may be when you're living closest to your
highest calling. Let yourself rest. The to-list will wait.

...........................................................................

*Lord, help me focus more on loving You and doing my best—and less on the
list.*

*As you do not know the path of the wind, or how the body is formed in a mother's womb, so you cannot understand the work of God, the Maker of all things.*

ECCLESIASTES 11:5

As children, we have big dreams for the future. Maybe we hoped we would be doctors, lawyers, or Disney princesses, or that we would live near the ocean. As we grow up, enter high school, go to college or get a job, and watch the years pass by, our lives can branch out in countless directions. Some of those childhood dreams come true, but many do not.

Does your life look completely different than you thought it would? Maybe you dreamed of being married or hoped to have more kids, but it just hasn't happened. Perhaps the career you worked so hard for just isn't fulfilling, or your financial security isn't what you'd hoped. Life is hard—especially when hopes and dreams are dashed.

If you feel this way, look to the Lord. He understands your frustrations and disappointments. And more than anything, He wants you to confide in Him and trust Him to lead you. God can transform those dashed hopes into part of His amazing plan—and you can have faith that He will fulfill His purpose for your life.

......................................................................

*God, I place my hopes and dreams for my life and my kids in Your steady and loving hands.*

*"In this world you will have trouble. But take*
*heart! I have overcome the world."*

JOHN 16:33

An old English proverb says, "Just when the caterpillar thought the world was over, it became a butterfly." The caterpillar hid away to put on wings of beauty and begin life renewed. But within a cocoon is a butterfly that is unaware of the outside world.

You may sometimes try to hide from pain and earthly troubles. Like spinning a cocoon, you may build walls around your heart. Use this time to spin new hopes and prepare to soar above the problems. Jesus guaranteed we would have problems in this world, so in our lives we should expect trouble. But He left us with a word of hope: He said He has overcome the world. Because the Spirit of God is in believers, we can overcome any difficult situation.

You cannot remain inside the cocoon forever. Eventually, you must come out and see the world. But use fresh eyes to see it from a new angle. In your dark resting place, seek to change by finding courage so you can sprout stronger wings. Hope's transformation will take place deep within your heart and soul.

..................................................................

*Father, thank You for the lesson of the butterfly, and thank You for the over-*
*coming power of Jesus that resides in me too.*

*Whatever is true, whatever is noble, whatever is right, whatever*
*is pure, whatever is lovely, whatever is admirable—if anything*
*is excellent or praiseworthy—think about such things.*

PHILIPPIANS 4:8

Anger. Jealousy. Self-contempt. Annoyance. How often do you think negatively? When your co-parent disagrees with a decision you made, do you let bitterness overtake you? Do you often find yourself thinking more negatively than positively throughout the day? If so, then perhaps it's time to change the way you think.

It's easy—all too easy—to wallow in self-pity or to fixate on your own anger or someone else's issues. But in doing so, you rob yourself of the joy found in all that is true, noble, right, pure, lovely, admirable, excellent, and praiseworthy. If your mind is a swirling realm of destructive thoughts, there's no room for anything else. That's a dark place to be. Think how much lighter it would feel to instead shift your focus—even if just a little bit at first—to the good that's around you.

Today, focus instead on what is true—that you are blessed by a God who loves you; that you are an amazing mom who is doing her best. Give your mind and body a break from negativity, and rest in the goodness of God.

...........................................................................

*Lord, when I'm feeling stuck in negativity, please help me to change my*
*attitude. Teach me to focus on whatever is pure and true.*

*The LORD your God is in your midst, a mighty one who will save; he will rejoice over you with gladness; he will quiet you by his love; he will exult over you with loud singing.*

ZEPHANIAH 3:17 ESV

The anticipation of the week to come is often challenging. Some people refer to this dread as the *Sunday scaries*. You've looked ahead at your schedule and all that you need to accomplish, and the demands of work or home life—or both—are exactly that: demanding. So if you already feel a little anxious and the week hasn't even begun yet, don't be discouraged!

Give yourself a few moments alone today. Sit in the quiet and remind yourself of these truths: God is with you and for you. He will never leave or forsake you. He rejoices over you with singing. He loves you. He gives strength to the weary. He wants to lift your burdens from you. And He tells you to rest.

Breathe in these promises from God, and let the hope they provide soak into your heart. Ask the Lord to make them clear to you throughout your week. Yes, the days may still be busy, and at times you might feel overwhelmed, but the Lord is on your side. Rest in the comfort of that truth today.

........................................................................

*Lord, speak Your truth into my life and throughout my days this week.*

*The LORD is my rock, my fortress and my deliverer;*
*my God is my rock, in whom I take refuge, my shield*
*and the horn of my salvation, my stronghold.*

PSALM 18:2

God doesn't always answer our prayers according to our timeline. Sometimes the answers just aren't what we'd expected or hoped. And sometimes, it may even feel like they aren't answered at all. But take heart that even if for now we know only in part, one day we will know fully, even as we are fully known (1 Corinthians 13:12).

God's timing matters. His reasons for when and how He answers our prayers may be beyond our ability to see at the moment, but that's because He sees the bigger picture. We can only live in this present moment, but God is omnipresent, living eternally in each and every moment. He sees how all the many pieces fit together, and He is working all these things together for your good.

Find rest in God's timing. Know that it may not be what you want, and you may have to lay down your own desires, but God is working for your eternal good. He is trustworthy. Have faith that His perfect answer is coming, in His perfect time.

...............................................................

*Father, help me trust that You answer my prayers perfectly and at the perfect time.*

*Weeping may last through the night, but*
*joy comes with the morning.*

PSALM 30:5 NLT

Today may be filled with pain that seems unbearable as tears flow freely. Loss and grief are difficult and may leave invisible scars that continue to plague you for a long time. It is difficult when you lose part of your heart because a loved one has passed on or you face devastating news that shakes you to the core.

The psalmist understood such emotional trauma. He knew that devastation was imminent because he had received a prophetic word from God. But once the event had passed, his weeping would be replaced with joy. He had hope for tomorrow because tomorrow promised to be free from pain.

Your pain may overwhelm your faith for a time. But people who love you will surround you and bring comfort. Take courage—your tears will not last forever. The God of all comfort is with you to comfort you. Your little ones still need your presence. They need you to be healthy and whole. So look forward to tomorrow and wait with hope. Tell God how you feel, and put your hopes in tomorrow, when your pain will be replaced with joy.

..................................................................

*Father, thank You for the joy and hope of tomorrow. Please comfort me so I can be present for my children.*

*We know and rely on the love God has for us. God is love.*
*Whoever lives in love lives in God, and God in them.*

I JOHN 4:16

If someone has wronged you, the pain can linger, even if the wrong-doing happened years ago. Whether a harsh comment, broken trust, or a stab in the back, everyone has experienced some sort of hurt in their lives. But if you're still holding on to that bitterness, pain, shame, or desire for revenge, it's time to let go. And in letting go, you will find freedom and peace.

First John 4:16 reminds us of how we are to live even amid the hurts and sorrows of this world: we are to live in love. Notice that God's Word doesn't say we are to live in love unless we've been hurt. No, we are to live in love—period.

As this truth sinks in, ask your Savior to show you how to let go of past hurts, and give yourself the time to do so. It may not happen overnight, but God can help you work through your pain. Pray that the Lord would replace those hurts with His love, joy, peace, kindness, and hope. For Christ can heal even the deepest wound and help you to love again.

......................................................................

*God, help me live with love, even when I've been wronged. Enable me to let go of any bitterness and resentment that have taken root in my heart.*

*"Consider the ravens: They do not sow or reap, they
have no storeroom or barn; yet God feeds them. And
how much more valuable you are than birds!"*

LUKE 12:24

That gift-giving holiday or vacation is over, and the bills are rolling in. Some are perhaps bigger than you were expecting. The soaring grocery spending reminds you that your kids are growing—and gobbling up all your food—very quickly, the repair bill to fix the car you must have for work is cringe-worthy, and your youngest just dropped your smartphone in the toilet. You're worried that your position at work may be made redundant, and the economy's not looking promising. The hits to your bank account always seem to come all at once.

Are you worrying about finances? Is your neck knotting with stress? Remember, the Lord wants you to give Him every burden and every concern—from the biggest to the smallest. Today, confess your worries to Him. He is the ultimate Provider, and He promises to take care of His children. Take a deep breath and remember that God wants you to be free from worry, even if your bank account looks bleak. Trust in Him.

..................................................................................

*God, I put my trust in You, the Provider of all good things. Please help me
provide for my family's needs.*

*The name of the LORD is a fortified tower;*
*the righteous run to it and are safe.*

PROVERBS 18:10

Imagine you're walking down a busy sidewalk. What would happen if you suddenly stopped and sat down to rest right in the middle of the sidewalk? You'd probably get bumped and knocked around. It wouldn't feel particularly restful because you'd be distracted—by the threat of imminent trampling!

That's often how it feels when we try to rest in this busy world. There's just so much going on. We sit down to pray, and the phone rings. We close the door for quiet time, and a child pounds on the door.

How can you sit still and find rest without getting trampled? First, get off the sidewalk. That means you need to set what boundaries you can and make your times of rest clear. Tell your kids, even if it means they get more screen time than you would prefer. Turn off your phone. Remove any distractions that you can. Then you can fully focus on being still before the Lord.

You can sit still in a busy world; it just takes some boundaries.

........................................................................

*Help me create time and space without distractions so I can sit still before You, Lord.*

...................................................................

...................................................................

...................................................................

...................................................................

...................................................................

...................................................................

...................................................................

...................................................................

...................................................................

...................................................................

...................................................................

...................................................................

...................................................................

...................................................................

...................................................................

...................................................................

...................................................................

...................................................................

...................................................................

*You, LORD, are our Father. We are the clay, you are*
*the potter; we are all the work of your hand.*

ISAIAH 64:8

I n the Bible, God has often been referred to as a potter, and we are
referred to as clay. It is a powerful metaphor that helps us understand
our relationship to God. A potter is a person who makes earthenware
from clay. The process can be grueling as the clay is spun and heated at
high temperatures.

Sometimes the pottery is broken while it is being shaped. But a
cracked or broken piece of pottery can be reused to make items stronger.
Potters grind broken pieces into grog and then add the grog to soft clay
to strengthen the mixture. The clay is still flexible but stronger because
of the broken particles. The right balance is needed before the potter
slaps the clay on the wheel and shapes it into a beautiful bowl, jar, or
other creation.

When your hope seems dashed or your dreams have shattered,
you can trust that God will redeem the brokenness. He will take the
shattered pieces, add the soft newness of hope, and help you to reshape
your dreams. Like the grog-infused clay, you can allow God to take the
broken remnants of your past to make you stronger.

..................................................................

*Father, even though dreams are sometimes shattered, I can trust that You*
*will reshape my hope.*

························································

························································

························································

························································

························································

························································

························································

························································

························································

························································

························································

························································

························································

························································

························································

························································

························································

*Praise the Lord, my soul, and forget not all his benefits—who forgives all your sins and heals all your diseases, who redeems your life from the pit and crowns you with love and compassion.*

Psalm 103:2–4

It's usually easy to tell when you are getting sick. You wake up with a sore throat, and you can't stop sneezing. You begin to feel aches and pains, and then the headache kicks in. You hit a wall and simply can't go another minute without a nap. That's when the chills start. When sickness is coming, your body gives you warning signs.

In the same way, when exhaustion is coming, your body will let you know. You may feel constantly fatigued, depressed, or discouraged. You may want to throw your alarm clock across the room when it wakes you in the morning. Listen to your body; it's time to start slowing down and allow yourself to rest.

Allow yourself to take a sick day from work if you can. Ask a coworker for help on that overwhelming project. Let your oldest child know that you need more help with chores around the house. Order a pizza for the kids rather than spending extra time in the kitchen. Say no to more obligations. If your body is telling you to rest, listen—and then rest.

．．．．．．．．．．．．．．．．．．．．．．．．．．．．．．．．．．．．．．．．．．．．．．．．．．．．．．．．．．．．．．．．．．．．．．．．．．

*Lord, my body feels so weary. Bless me with rest today.*

*Unless the Lord builds the house, the builders labor in vain.*

Psalm 127:1

*P*roductivity is a word used proudly. The more we get done in the day or week, the more accomplished we feel. Long workdays are often expected, and working on the weekends is the norm. Even when you're home from work, many employers expect you to answer work-related emails and be on call. In a society where productivity is king and rest is dismissed as unnecessary, how do we find respite from the constant going, going, going?

We simply have to do it. We rest. We rest without hesitation and without guilt. We take time off from work and obligations to enjoy our families, our God, and His creation. Rest is essential; our culture just doesn't want to admit it.

You may feel as if your world will come crashing down if you're not productive. You might feel as if it's impossible to rest if your to-do list isn't finished. You might even feel lazy or worthless if you take time to rest. Push those thoughts out of your head because rest is essential— God can handle everything else.

....................................................................

*God, I am afraid to rest and feel unproductive. Show me that when I rest, my kids, my work, and I all benefit.*

........................................................................

........................................................................

........................................................................

........................................................................

........................................................................

........................................................................

........................................................................

........................................................................

........................................................................

........................................................................

........................................................................

........................................................................

........................................................................

........................................................................

........................................................................

........................................................................

........................................................................

........................................................................

........................................................................

........................................................................

*On a good day, enjoy yourself; on a bad day, examine
your conscience. God arranges for both kinds of days
so that we won't take anything for granted.*

ECCLESIASTES 7:14 MSG

When you look back over the days that have passed, you may see times of pain and grief that you never expected. But you will also see times of joy and blessings that you never anticipated as well. Your review of those days may cause you to realize that it was best that those days unfolded one at a time. You can trust all your tomorrows to God. But today has the opportunity for living and enjoying present moments. Today your hope is alive and is all you can handle. Jesus said the troubles that we experience are only for that day. Tomorrow has not come, so we do not know what it will bring. The strength that you have is for today and not tomorrow.

Between the soft lights of dawn with the newness of the morning dew and the setting of the sun with its glorious colors, there is enough time to fill with work, pleasure, cares, and dreams. Enjoy every moment to the fullest. You cannot make time move any faster, so do not try to rush it, and do not waste time worrying about tomorrow. Relish the glorious moment-by-moment unfolding of today.

..................................................................

*Dear God, thank You for today. Bless me to live to the fullest, and help me
to let tomorrow take care of itself.*

*As God's chosen people, holy and dearly loved, clothe yourselves*
*with compassion, kindness, humility, gentleness and patience.*

COLOSSIANS 3:12

L aughter and smiles transform a face. When you see someone you know looking sad, you may ask what is wrong and try to respond with a funny story or cheerful words to lift their spirits. An act of compassion is not a lost art, but it may not be as prevalent as it once was. The culture and times have caused many people to be leery of others. When once a person could receive help from strangers, today the misdeeds of others have caused innocent people to suffer rather than accept help from strangers or watch someone else suffer rather than extend compassion.

Sometimes you have to take a chance and be different by being the compassionate person God has called you to be. Compassionate people ease the pain of those who are suffering. You may send cards or flowers and pray when someone you love is hurting. That is showing compassion. And you have likely received sympathy and tokens of love when you have gone through a difficult time. That is also compassion. Compassionate people are those who God uses in our lives to remind us how dearly loved we are.

...............................................................................

*God, give me a compassionate heart so that I can be used by You to uplift*
*the spirits of others.*

*"No longer do I call you servants, for the servant does not know
what his master is doing; but I have called you friends, for all
that I have heard from my Father I have made known to you."*

JOHN 15:15 ESV

There are some friends who just get you. When you see one another, even after months or years apart, you simply pick up where you left off. There's no discomfort and no need for small talk. Spending time with a friend like this feels easy and comfortable, like a warm hug personified. Those types of friends are keepers.

Jesus is one of those friends; in fact, He's the perfect Friend. You might confide a lot in your closest friends, but only Jesus knows all your sins, insecurities, and embarrassments—and He loves you unconditionally. He sees you fail every single day, and He still wants to spend time with you. Amazing, isn't it? It's similar to how you feel about your own children.

If you haven't spoken to Jesus in a while, you can still go to Him with confidence. See Him running toward you, eager to welcome you back; feel Him embrace you tenderly; and relax in the realization that He is faithful to you. Jesus' friendship provides respite for our striving, searching, discontented souls. What a friend we have in Him.

..............................................................................

*You are the best friend I've ever had, Jesus. You're always here for me.
Thank You.*

*Forgetting what is behind and straining toward what*
*is ahead, I press on toward the goal to win the prize for*
*which God has called me heavenward in Christ Jesus.*

PHILIPPIANS 3:13–14

How do you feel about running? If you're like most people, you either love it or you hate it—there is no in between. It takes perseverance to keep moving forward when your legs are tired, your lungs are burning, and the road is all uphill.

Paul used the analogy of running to describe his spiritual goal. In verse 10 of Philippians 3, he said he wanted to know Jesus. This was a noble goal that many during his time thought they had already accomplished. But Paul realized he had not arrived at his destination. Therefore, he said with determination that he would "press on" (v. 12). There was no looking back. He had to persevere so that he could finish his race and win the prize, which is heaven (Luke 6:23).

What goal are you currently working toward? Are any old habits or previous mistakes tripping you up? Isaiah 43:18 tells us, "Forget the former things; do not dwell on the past." It may be time to let go of previous missteps and fix your eyes on what's ahead. Keep pressing forward.

· · · · · · · · · · · · · · · · · · · · · · · · · · · · · · · · · · · · · · · · · · · · · · · · · ·

*Dear God, I am pressing forward to accomplish what You have placed in*
*my heart. Keep me focused so I can reach my goal.*

*Jesus asked him, "Judas, are you betraying*
*the Son of Man with a kiss?"*

LUKE 22:48

Losing an important relationship can be painful, especially when it is the result of betrayal. Betrayal cuts you to the core as the trust or faith that you had in someone else is shattered. The trauma can create such great sorrow that only time and choosing forgiveness can bring healing.

Jesus looked at Judas and questioned him about a kiss that signaled Judas's deception. A kiss usually communicates affection, but Judas's gesture toward Jesus was his betrayal. Judas's deceptive heart was revealed in an instant and launched a sequence of events that resulted in the death of our Savior. But all was not lost; Jesus's death wasn't the end. After three days, He rose from the dead! On several occasions thereafter, He met with His disciples and others. He shared new life and new hope through the good news of His resurrection. In spite of Judas's betrayal, hope has changed the world and continues to exist. Even today it continues to impact every area of our lives. Recognize the power of hope in your life, and allow it to undergird the hope you have in others.

...................................................................

*Dear God, thank You for the hope You have provided through the resurrection of Jesus. Help me to forgive as Jesus did and to grow stronger, despite betrayal.*

*"Take my yoke upon you. Let me teach you, because I am humble and gentle at heart, and you will find rest for your souls. For my yoke is easy to bear, and the burden I give you is light."*

MATTHEW 11:29–30 NLT

Have you ever tried everything you could think of to work out a problem and nothing fixed it? You may feel exhausted and do not know how you can continue, but that does not mean you have exhausted all the possibilities. Jesus said if you are weary, He will give you rest. Sometimes you may become weighed down by responsibilities, work, or whatever you are doing to accomplish your goals. Jesus compared your burden to being harnessed to a yoke. A yoke is a wooden frame used for carrying a load or fastening animals together so they can do double the work together. Jesus said if your burden is heavy, then you should put down your yoke and put His yoke on because His yoke is easy.

When you feel hopeless and cannot find a solution, take a break and look to Jesus. It might be time to refresh your mind and spirit with rest. Indulge in a favorite activity, or visit a favorite spot. Relax, pray, and let your troubles go. Then remember that there is always another possibility, another idea to try. Jesus will lead you every step of the way. Once you are relaxed, have recharged your mind, and have renewed your spirit, take a new look, but this time look with Jesus.

*Dear God, thank You that I can go to Jesus for rest when I am weary.*

*How good and pleasant it is when God's*
*people live together in unity!*
PSALM 133:1

Who do you go to when you have a prayer request? Or when you're having a hard day? Or you simply need help? If certain individuals pop into your head, those people are your community. They're the ones who can support you in tangible ways—and they're the ones with whom you can risk being vulnerable.

Being vulnerable isn't a comfortable feeling in today's do-it-yourself society. But once you risk being honest and vulnerable with someone, chances are that person will risk being honest and vulnerable with you too.

Perhaps you've just had surgery and need help with meals; ask your community. Maybe you need help with a colicky baby; ask your community. Or perhaps you're weary of searching for a job; ask your community for prayers and help networking. Be brave enough to risk asking for help, to risk being vulnerable. And when you feel rested, be sure to return the favor. In this way we can "carry each other's burdens, and in this way you will fulfill the law of Christ" (Galatians 6:2).

..............................................................................

*Lord, it's hard to ask for help. Give me the courage to be vulnerable with my community.*

....................................................................................

....................................................................................

....................................................................................

....................................................................................

....................................................................................

....................................................................................

....................................................................................

....................................................................................

....................................................................................

....................................................................................

....................................................................................

....................................................................................

....................................................................................

....................................................................................

....................................................................................

....................................................................................

....................................................................................

....................................................................................

*Be joyful in hope, patient in affliction, faithful in prayer.*
ROMANS 12:12

We love uplifting, inspirational stories of people who have overcome challenging times. After tragedies, natural disasters, or other newsworthy events, we see uplifting reports of the individuals who have been devastated but have carried on.

The main reason many of us do not buckle under the weight of our circumstances is because of the hope that is in our hearts. Characteristically, just like faith, hope is strengthened by adversity. The experience of having gone through something difficult toughens our resolve so that we believe we are going to be okay.

In verse 12 of Romans 12, Paul tried to help us understand that going through difficult times was no excuse to abandon hope. We should remain joyful in hope as we wait in anticipation for God's promises to be fulfilled, with the greatest promise being heaven.

When you experience difficulty, you have a choice. One option is to hide in a dark place away from the world, or you can face the adversity head on, knowing that you are not alone. God is there. Just reach out to Him in prayer. The hope that He has placed in your heart will see you through. And the next time you endure a trial, your hope will be stronger.

.....................................................................

*Dear God, thank You for hope that is strengthened through every trial.*

........................................................................

........................................................................

........................................................................

........................................................................

........................................................................

........................................................................

........................................................................

........................................................................

........................................................................

........................................................................

........................................................................

........................................................................

........................................................................

........................................................................

........................................................................

........................................................................

........................................................................

*The LORD gives strength to his people; the
LORD blesses his people with peace.*

PSALM 29:11

We like to stay connected. We like to know where our kids are, what our friends are up to, and what the latest news headlines are. And all this information is available with the touch of a screen.

But staying connected can become an obsession. Do you panic if you don't have your phone? Are you constantly scrolling through your social media feeds? Are you reading news headlines more than your Bible? It's easy to get caught up in the trap of being overconnected. It can become a case of too much of a good thing—it's all about maintaining a healthy balance with our screen time, much like you try to do for your children.

To find rest—the kind that refreshes mind, body, and spirit—you may need to unplug. Turn off your phone. Set aside your screens and look, instead, into the eyes of your kids. Listen to the wind in the trees, and laugh at a silly joke. Unplugging is hard to do, but it is so beneficial. And once you try it, you may not want to plug back in.

...........................................................................

*Lord, help me seek rest and refreshment in Your presence, not in online noise and busyness.*

*Cast all your anxiety on him because he cares for you.*

I Peter 5:7

As a mom, you may feel predisposed to worry. You might even think it helps prepare or brace you for difficult situations—but really it just drains your energy on imagined scenarios that may not even play out in the ways you think they will.

However, for years medical doctors have expounded on the detrimental medical issues that result from too much worry. They contend that during the waking hours, a worrier is subject to panic attacks, and at night, a lack of sleep. Worrying can impact your daily life so much that you cannot function. The doctors' major concerns are that worry can cause physical illnesses such as heart attacks, high blood pressure, and other problems.

The apostle Peter encouraged his readers to get rid of worry altogether by casting their cares on Jesus. If you hold on to worries, you're perhaps unconsciously communicating that you do not trust God. But God is your hope, and He really does care. He is able to create balance in your life, including your work, your relationships, and especially with your kids. So spend your days loving your family well and worrying less. If worry breaks through, let it go by casting your concerns on Jesus.

........................................................................

*Dear God, I give You my worries and concerns. Thank You for caring enough to take them.*

*[There is] a time to weep and a time to laugh,*
*a time to mourn and a time to dance.*

ECCLESIASTES 3:4

There's an adage that says, "If you are too busy to laugh, you are too busy." There should always be time to laugh and appreciate life, especially during these short years with your kids still in the home. Days without laughter could mean you are too busy. Busyness is caused by saying yes to too many requests of your time and by underestimating the time you will need to fulfill your commitments.

Overscheduling can be draining and stressful—for both you and your kids. Do you think it may be time to pull back?

Decide which activities are priorities for your family, and make a decision to say no before you are asked to do something that doesn't fit those priorities. If guilty feelings start to creep in, give them the boot.

Let laughter be your test for busyness. Fueling your family life with laughter recharges your body and spirit. Place funny things your kids have said and silly pictures of them on your refrigerator. At the end of the day, reflect on those comments and priceless moments. Let laughter bring you enjoyment and be the catalyst for more laughs.

*Lord, when I am tempted to overschedule myself and my kids, please remind me to prioritize and create balance. Help me to enjoy these memories with my family.*

LORD, *you establish peace for us; all that we*
*have accomplished you have done for us.*

ISAIAH 26:12

When Jesus said from the cross, "It is finished," He paid the price for your sin once and for all (John 19:30). He gave His life, the ultimate sacrifice, so that you wouldn't have to bear the punishment. Are you living in the freedom of that?

Too many Christians are still trying to earn God's favor by living perfectly. But that's impossible; and, thankfully, God doesn't expect us to be perfect. Instead, He calls us to trust Him completely and to believe in the finished work of the cross.

Can you allow yourself to rest in the work of the cross today? Can you let go of the urge to continually prove yourself and your faithfulness to God? Can you let go of the desire to be the perfect woman and mom? Can you accept that God could never love you any more or any less than He already does?

Today, surrender your quest for perfection, and simply praise God for what He's done for you. Let your life be marked by complete reliance on the work of the cross. Rest in the peace of your salvation.

......................................................................

*Jesus, thank You for paying the price for my sin. When I'm striving for*
*perfection, please help me to rest in that peace.*

..............................................................................

..............................................................................

..............................................................................

..............................................................................

..............................................................................

..............................................................................

..............................................................................

..............................................................................

..............................................................................

..............................................................................

..............................................................................

..............................................................................

..............................................................................

..............................................................................

..............................................................................

..............................................................................

..............................................................................

..............................................................................

..............................................................................

..............................................................................

*Evening, morning and noon I cry out in*
*distress, and he hears my voice.*

PSALM 55:17

Chronic pain is a harsh reality for many people, and possibly for you too. Maybe you suffer from chronic migraines or have an autoimmune disease. We live in a fallen world, and nothing we do can prevent all suffering and pain.

The book of Luke tells the story of a woman who had suffered from bleeding for twelve years, but "no one could heal her" (8:43). The woman approached Jesus in a crowd, hoping and believing that He was different. As she reached out in faith and touched the edge of His clothing, she was healed immediately! We don't always get instantaneous answers to prayer like this. But Jesus healed the woman, called her daughter, and blessed her, and He wants to heal and bless all His children.

Your suffering causes you to empathize with others and creates an awareness of how others feel when they are in pain. When you live bravely and cope well with your pain, you can be an example to others that pain does not have to rule their lives. The greater hope is that God hears when you cry out to Him. There will be no pain or tears in heaven, but when you suffer while here on earth, you are never alone.

........................................................................

*Dear Lord, thank You that You hear me when I call to You in distress. Help me to remember that I am never alone because You are always there for me.*

*This is the day that the LORD has made;*
*let us rejoice and be glad in it.*
PSALM 118:24 ESV

So often, at the end of a day, we feel defeated by everything that we didn't do. We forgot to turn in our child's field trip permission form, we didn't finish those meeting notes, and we're having frozen chicken nuggets for dinner again. And our to-do list? It grew.

Instead of focusing on the day's defeats, why not rest in today's triumphs? Grab a pad of paper and write down everything you did do—from the smallest to the largest task. Maybe you fed all three kids and got them to the bus stop on time. Perhaps you nailed the big project at work. Did you encourage a friend, laugh until you cried, or point someone toward Christ today? You can also think about the things you *didn't* do that were a triumph—not losing your patience with your co-parent, not getting into it with that driver during rush hour, not criticizing yourself throughout the day. Write it all down.

Today's defeats can be frustrating, but don't let them dominate your feelings about the day. Focus on today's accomplishments. Tomorrow is a new day, but today was far from a complete waste. Celebrate your successes, and rest in knowing that God is glorified by your efforts.

........................................................................

*Help me celebrate today's triumphs, God, and rest in the glory they bring*
*Your name.*

........................................................................................................

........................................................................................................

........................................................................................................

........................................................................................................

........................................................................................................

........................................................................................................

........................................................................................................

........................................................................................................

........................................................................................................

........................................................................................................

........................................................................................................

........................................................................................................

........................................................................................................

........................................................................................................

........................................................................................................

........................................................................................................

........................................................................................................

........................................................................................................

........................................................................................................

*"Do not worry about tomorrow, for tomorrow will worry about itself. Each day has enough trouble of its own."*

MATTHEW 6:34

God knows the future—how long you will live, which careers your children will grow up to pursue, every achievement, and every failure. He is intricately involved in every single moment in your life and your kids' lives, and He is working each of those moments together for His glory. Even so, everything that is still to come can feel scary.

That's because, for us humans, the future is uncertain. No one knows when our earthly lives will end, if that loved one will survive cancer, or if a child will make good choices. Nobody can predict the job market or stock market or when natural disasters and national tragedies will strike. We don't even know how long our planet will last or if our children will live to see children of their own.

No, you can't know the future, but the One who calls you His beloved child does know. The One who calms your fears and wipes away your tears knows what you will need to face what's coming. Find comfort in knowing that the One who holds the future in His hands also holds you and your kids.

...................................................................

*Father, when I am afraid of what may come, please remind me that You hold the future in Your trustworthy hands.*

*Jesus often withdrew to lonely places and prayed.*

LUKE 5:16

Think about your daily schedule. Do you have a time slot specifically reserved for rest? You may have penciled in time for picking up the kids, taking an online class, making dinner, or working, but does the word *rest* seem like a foreign concept?

Maybe that's because rest is about so much more than sleep. Of course, single moms need that too! But true rest is about finding peace—allowing quiet moments for rejuvenation and renewal.

Rest doesn't just fall into your lap, and it won't tap you on your shoulder during a busy day to remind you to take a break. Downtime needs to be sought out. It needs to be carved into each day, week, and month, and it needs to be intentional.

Today's culture is busy. Your life is busy. But that doesn't mean you cannot rest; it just needs to be added to your calendar. Just as you make time to attend your child's school program or visit family at Christmastime, rest needs to be scheduled. Try waking up fifteen minutes earlier to sit in the quiet before your kids are up. Instead of browsing social media, take a walk or sit outside and breathe deeply. Seek rest, and you will be rewarded—mind, body, and soul.

...............................................................................

*Lord, help me set aside quiet time each day to refresh my spirit, even when it seems impossible.*

*If you do what the LORD wants, he will make*

*certain each step you take is sure.*

PSALM 37:23 CEV

When you were growing up, did your family ever take road trips? Did you gaze out the window and play games like I Spy? Riding along on a winding country road, you would discover a different surprise around every turn as the scenery changed along the way.

Your journey in life is like traveling on a winding road. Each day is a bend in the road that is filled with laughter, pain, lessons, celebrations, and special moments. Occasionally, there may be bumps in the road. But you can rest assured that when you delight in God, He will establish your steps. Furthermore, God has promised that when you face an obstacle, the "LORD will hold your hand, and if you stumble, you still won't fall" (Psalm 37:24 CEV).

The turns in your life aren't dead ends. They are little twists that allow you to see a new phase of your life unfold. Find reasons to be grateful for new opportunities or challenges that help you reach your dreams, and remember the One who travels with you. You may want to keep a journal as you journey along the way and look back at your journal entries so you can be reminded of how God has established each of your days.

...............................................................................

*God, thank You for traveling with my kids and me on my life's journey. I am full of hope knowing that You are guiding me along the way.*

*Thanks be to God for his indescribable gift!*

2 CORINTHIANS 9:15

Sometimes you receive a call, an email, or a text that says your plans have been canceled. You have been blessed with an unexpected opening in your day, and your calendar looks a little less hectic. What do you do?

If at all possible, resist the urge to fill that opening with the next thing on your list. Pause before you grab your phone or laptop, and ask yourself, *Do I need this unexpected time to rejuvenate and rest? Is this time an opportunity for a relaxing family day? Could it be a gift?*

When your schedule opens up, it's easy to react as if you were a corporation or business, quickly filling that empty time. Instead, try to approach your calendar with a more human, less busy-mom mindset. Let that space stay open. Don't try to cross a few more things off your checklist, set up that appointment, or cram in one more activity for your kids.

Instead, stop and consider your opportunities for downtime. Enjoy an extra-long, hot shower. Sit and drink your coffee while it's still hot—the first time. When you receive a gift of unexpected time, allow yourself to relax.

.................................................................

*When my calendar opens up unexpectedly, Lord, point me toward rest instead of my to-do list.*

*You created my inmost being; you knit me*
*together in my mother's womb.*

PSALM 139:13

G od's love holds the power to change you from the inside out. It is a transforming power to make you brand new. God will not change you against your will; after all, He gave you free will. We are the only creatures on earth God has made who can refuse to do something that He has asked us to do. He made us that way because He wants us to freely love Him back. Even if we refuse to love God, He will continue to love us and will remind us about His perfect ways.

God chose to create you and love you before your birth. He put you together while your mother was carrying you. He has placed part of Himself in every person, so He knows all about you and relates to you. He responds to your prayers and wants to help you to change for the better.

When you accept His love, you learn more about Him. You begin to reflect His love and goodness. Then others will see His Spirit within you and will be drawn to His love. They, too, will learn that God knows them and has loved them since before they were born.

..............................................................................

*Dear God, thank You for creating me with such care. Help me to be transformed by Your love.*

......................................................................

......................................................................

......................................................................

......................................................................

......................................................................

......................................................................

......................................................................

......................................................................

......................................................................

......................................................................

......................................................................

......................................................................

......................................................................

......................................................................

......................................................................

......................................................................

......................................................................

......................................................................

......................................................................

......................................................................

*Because of the LORD's great love we are not consumed,*
*for his compassions never fail. They are new*
*every morning; great is your faithfulness.*

LAMENTATIONS 3:22–23

When hopelessness tries to creep in, it is time for revival. In overcoming, you gain confidence that you can continue and not let difficulties win. The Bible refers to these mishaps as "afflictions." The word *affliction* suggests great pain and suffering. This hopeless state can be brought on by illness, hurt, catastrophe, loss, and failure, among other events.

Do not allow these difficulties to make you feel hopeless or overwhelmed. Do not give hopelessness the attention that it demands. In the book of Lamentations, you receive the revival that you need. It reveals that God's great love never fails. Every morning when you wake up, His love and compassion are still strong, even in the midst of hopelessness.

When you take a deep breath and slow down to look at a problem, you may think of another approach. With each little conquest and with the love of God to spur you on, hope recovers, and you breathe a little easier again. Smile and rejoice when you give new life to your hopes and revive your dreams.

......................................................................

*God, thank You for Your compassion that is my focus and my revival for*
*overcoming the struggles of the day.*

·····································································

·····································································

·····································································

·····································································

·····································································

·····································································

·····································································

·····································································

·····································································

·····································································

·····································································

·····································································

·····································································

·····································································

·····································································

·····································································

·····································································

·····································································

·····································································

·····································································

*Am I now trying to win the approval of human beings, or of
God? Or am I trying to please people? If I were still trying
to please people, I would not be a servant of Christ.*

GALATIANS 1:10

'm not mad; I'm just disappointed. Did your heart just twinge reading those words? Maybe you remember the sting of hearing those words from a parent, teacher, or coach. Some people so dread disappointing others that they strive to please everyone all the time. They work and work and then work some more to make sure everyone is happy.

But trying to please everyone is exhausting—and impossible. Admit it: you can't make everyone happy. It's essential that you set priorities for yourself and your family and create boundaries. Of course, you can say yes to some things, but it's not your duty to say yes to all things. Sometimes you simply need to say no to others and say yes to God and yourself. Putting God first and giving some priority to nourishing your own body and soul are key components for creating balance.

Do you need to put a pause on pleasing others today? Ask the Lord to help you focus on pleasing Him first and to give you the discernment and strength to set necessary boundaries.

........................................................................

*Jesus, help me establish healthy boundaries and remind me to focus on You
first and foremost.*

........................................................................

........................................................................

........................................................................

........................................................................

........................................................................

........................................................................

........................................................................

........................................................................

........................................................................

........................................................................

........................................................................

........................................................................

........................................................................

........................................................................

........................................................................

........................................................................

........................................................................

........................................................................

........................................................................

........................................................................

*"He himself bore our sins" in his body on the cross, so*
*that we might die to sins and live for righteousness;*
*"by his wounds you have been healed."*

I Peter 2:24

What's weighing heavily on your mind today? Is it the sin that so easily entangles you (Hebrews 12:1)? Are you waiting for the doctor to reveal some test results? Are you worried about your son or daughter, your parents or sibling? Do you feel as if you're in over your head as a single mom? Maybe you feel unloved, unwanted, or lonely. Whatever you may be going through, it's not too heavy for the cross.

Write down your burdens today—all of them. Whether you're worried about your sickly dog, the report you need to write, the continual car repairs, your child's performance in school, or your grandmother's cancer, write it down. Then picture yourself bringing this list of burdens and worries to the cross and leaving it there.

Jesus will take that list from you. He wants to carry your burdens for you. He wants to relieve you of the fears you're holding on to and the shame you may be feeling. He wants you to leave everything at the cross and find rest.

...................................................................

*Father, thank You for bearing my burdens. Remind me to leave them with*
*You.*

*"I have come that they may have life, and have it to the full."*
JOHN 10:10

A s you look ahead at the path of your life, you may realize it is a long journey. But stopping to appreciate the beautiful moments along the way will add joy to your experience. This is the kind of thing you do only if you relish the wonder of being alive and enjoying God's creation. This is a deeper experience of life than merely goal-reaching. God wants us to enjoy abundant experiences along the way.

Jesus lived the world's most significant journey, but He stopped to cherish children and bless them (Mark 10:16). He sent His disciples and friends away from Him so that He could commune alone with His Father. He paused to become acquainted with a man in a tree as He passed through Jericho (Luke 19:5). At a feast, Jesus appreciated the beautiful act one follower performed with her alabaster jar of perfume (Mark 14:3–9). His parables showed how observant He was of all that is fascinating in nature, the world, and the human spirit.

In your journey, take time to enjoy everything around you. Relish this season with your kids. Take in the beauty of a sunset, the feeling of sand between your toes, or the sound of birds singing. These are the moments that string together to create a meaningful life.

..................................................................

*God, in the busyness of life, give me eyes to see and enjoy the wonder of the beauty around me.*

*What is seen is temporary, but what is unseen is eternal.*

2 Corinthians 4:18

O n wintry days when you have to bundle up to stay warm, you may dream about hot summer days of walking along the beach or sitting in the sun and reading a book. You may be miserable in the cold, but it won't be long before those sunny days arrive again.

The apostle Paul taught that our hope is in the unseen. He had experienced a life of hardship, suffering, and persecution and was eventually (most likely) martyred. But Paul had his sights set on eternity because he recognized that what he was going through was not all there was to life. He recognized that he would one day live in a better place. He would spend eternity with God.

When things look bleak, you can set your sights on what God has for you in the future. This hope lets you believe in what is unseen. An image in your mind can draw your thoughts from current circumstances and mentally transport you to another time and place. It helps you to discover the anticipation of believing in future possibilities.

If you are shivering with doubts and fears, know that this season will pass. Know, too, that God is preparing a heavenly place for you that will outshine any dark moment.

....................................................................

*Father, though the days are sometimes dark, I look forward to the future
You have for me. It is an unseen hope.*

*I lie down and sleep; I wake again, because the LORD sustains me.*

PSALM 3:5

When you imagine the ultimate bedroom oasis, what comes to mind? If you look at photos of a fancy hotel room or even pictures in a home magazine, the bedrooms are typically serene and calm. They aren't cluttered, and they have crisp, white sheets on a large, luxurious bed, with sunlight filtering through fingerprint-free windows.

When you walk into your own bedroom, does it evoke the same feelings of peace and serenity? Or do you trip over a laundry basket of clothes that need to be put away, some kids' toys, and a few discarded books just to reach your bed? If your bedroom—the place where you're supposed to go for rest—isn't a haven for finding peace, it may be time to make a few small changes.

These changes don't have to cost a thing! First, tidy up and declutter your bedroom. Dust your blinds, vacuum your curtains, and wash your bedding. Light a soothing candle. Make it a place where you can breathe in peace, not a place where you look around and see only more undone to-dos. If you make your bedroom a sanctuary and a retreat, your body and mind will be better freed to rest. Create your own oasis—it's a totally free act of self-care.

...................................................................

*Lord, help me create a haven of rest for myself, a place where I can go at the end of a long day to refresh and renew so I can be at my best for my kids.*

....................................................................................

....................................................................................

....................................................................................

....................................................................................

....................................................................................

....................................................................................

....................................................................................

....................................................................................

....................................................................................

....................................................................................

....................................................................................

....................................................................................

....................................................................................

....................................................................................

....................................................................................

....................................................................................

....................................................................................

....................................................................................

....................................................................................

*"Indeed, the very hairs of your head are all numbered. Don't*
*be afraid; you are worth more than many sparrows."*

LUKE 12:7

Consider how much time you spend each day thinking or worrying about other people, especially about what someone else has said or may have thought about you. Do these types of things consume your thoughts? It may be helpful to know that most of the time other people are not thinking about you as much as you believe. They are too focused on their own personal worries and life concerns to think about you.

But with God, His thoughts are always centered on you with love. He would have sent His Son to die for you even if you were the only person on earth. The human head holds an average of one hundred thousand hairs, and each day it loses fifty to one hundred of those hairs. God cares enough to count the hairs on your head. Your heavenly Father also listens to your every thought, sees each tear you cry, and cares about what is hidden in your heart.

You don't need to be afraid or dismayed about what others may or may not think of you. God lovingly cares for the sparrows by His hand, and yet He values you far more than the sparrows. He wants to fill you with hope because He cherishes you.

...........................................................................

*Lord, thank You for lovingly caring for me. You know everything about me.*
*Thank You for valuing me as Your creation.*

........................................................................

........................................................................

........................................................................

........................................................................

........................................................................

........................................................................

........................................................................

........................................................................

........................................................................

........................................................................

........................................................................

........................................................................

........................................................................

........................................................................

........................................................................

........................................................................

*Why is light given to a man whose way is hidden?*

JOB 3:23 ESV

Too often hearts are broken and dreams are shattered. In the book of Job, many questions were asked and many were implied, some by Job, others by his friends and his wife. They asked questions such as these: *Why do the righteous suffer? How can God allow the righteous to suffer?* But the most frequently asked question centered on why.

"Why?" is a natural question to ask when you are suffering or in pain. When Job asked why, God didn't answer him directly. Instead, He responded by asking Job more questions. He asked, "Where were you when I laid the earth's foundation?" (38:4). This question humbled Job because he realized his own feeble stature, and he learned that despite heartbreak, God had the power to make everything brand new.

When Job looked beyond the whys of his heartbreak and instead trusted in and found comfort in God, God gave Job new hope and restored his life. In heaven, there will be no pain and wickedness, but until then, here on earth, suffering will exist. Even when you don't understand why God allows some difficult experiences to happen, you know without a shadow of a doubt that He will continue to comfort you, strengthen you, and give you renewed hope.

......................................................................

*Lord, when I don't understand why You allow suffering or difficulties in my life, please remind me of Your love and care.*

......................................................................................

......................................................................................

......................................................................................

......................................................................................

......................................................................................

......................................................................................

......................................................................................

......................................................................................

......................................................................................

......................................................................................

......................................................................................

......................................................................................

......................................................................................

......................................................................................

......................................................................................

......................................................................................

......................................................................................

......................................................................................

*The peace of God, which transcends all understanding,*
*will guard your hearts and your minds in Christ Jesus.*

PHILIPPIANS 4:7

As a woman and a mom who needs to remember so many details and dates, does your brain feel like it's overloaded? Each day your mind stores and sorts through experiences, comments, and information. Modern society has saturated our senses with distractions. Today hundreds of television channels, video games, electronic devices, social media, and billboards compete for our attention. Without realizing what we are doing, we voluntarily open up our minds and allow these forces to invade our thoughts.

But God calls for us to take care of our minds. We are advised to put our focus on those things that are noble, right, pure, lovely, and admirable (Philippians 4:8).

If too much is going on inside your brain, it is time for a break. Turn off the radio during your commute. Don't turn on the television for background noise. Silence your phone notifications for a few hours. Create spaces so your mind can unwind. Being reflective allows you to be mindful of what you are allowing to fill your thoughts so you can align your thoughts with God's will.

*God, help me be intentional in my thought life so that my mind focuses on the things of You.*

........................................................................

........................................................................

........................................................................

........................................................................

........................................................................

........................................................................

........................................................................

........................................................................

........................................................................

........................................................................

........................................................................

........................................................................

........................................................................

........................................................................

........................................................................

........................................................................

........................................................................

> *"For where your treasure is, there your heart will be also."*
>
> MATTHEW 6:21

Wouldn't it be great if money really did grow on trees? Then every time you needed—or simply wanted—something, you could walk outside, grab some money, and head for the store. It would certainly make your kids' Christmas wish lists easier to handle! Life, however, doesn't work that way, and that's probably a good thing. If you had all the money you ever wanted, you might never learn how to rely on the Lord.

So often it's the people who have the least money who have the deepest trust in God. Why? Because they've seen Him provide for them over and over again. When we feel as if we're providing for ourselves, we risk beginning to trust in ourselves and in our own abilities instead of trusting in God, the ultimate Provider.

Instead of a money tree, the Lord has given you something far greater: through Christ, you've been given the gift of a relationship with the One who created the trees. Rest in that truth, and trust Him to supply all your needs.

...........................................................................

*Lord, may I fully rest in Your provision instead of trusting in my own abilities.*

*"Tomorrow is to be a day of sabbath rest,*
*a holy sabbath to the LORD."*
EXODUS 16:23

S ometimes the most spiritual thing you can do is take a nap. Pastors and speakers have echoed this sentiment through the years, but how often do you follow their advice?

Our bodies need physical rest. If we keep pushing and pushing and pushing, we'll burn out at work, we'll burn out at home, and we'll burn out our bodies. Physical rest is necessary for us to function fully and wholly.

Consider taking a nap today. Going to church, visiting with extended family, or going on an outing with your kids are all wonderful and perhaps even necessary parts of your Sabbath days, but don't discount the spiritual value of an afternoon nap. Challenge yourself to carve out a naptime today. It may seem self-indulgent, but it can actually be the best thing for your spiritual, physical, and emotional health. When you're napping, you're following the Sabbath command: to rest.

........................................................................

*Lord, remind me that taking a nap may be the most spiritual thing this*
*tired mama can do today.*

*As for you, you meant evil against me, but God meant it for good.*

GENESIS 50:20 ESV

The book of Genesis reveals that God gave Joseph dreams and a vision to do great things. Joseph knew that God had a plan for him. Being sold into slavery by his brothers did not seem to fit the plan. But although Joseph's brothers intended harm against him, God turned everything around for Joseph's good. God knew ahead of time what would happen, and He had already devised a plan to make Joseph a ruler in Egypt.

Are you stressed because your life seems out of sorts? Are you currently in the midst of a seemingly hopeless situation? Remember that God always has a plan, even when the unexpected happens or when things go wrong. God took care of Joseph when his brothers wanted to get rid of him. He used their actions to fulfill a plan that He had ordained. Their actions became tools in His hands to fulfill His purpose for Joseph.

If God did that for Joseph, He will certainly do the same for you. He ordered your steps a long time ago and will keep you in His plan, even when others intend to harm you or your circumstances become difficult. Joseph never lost hope, nor should you. Remain faithful to God, and determine to pursue His will. Remember that God is in control.

........................................................................

*God, thank You that You know all about me and can use any situation for good.*

.................................................................................

.................................................................................

.................................................................................

.................................................................................

.................................................................................

.................................................................................

.................................................................................

.................................................................................

.................................................................................

.................................................................................

.................................................................................

.................................................................................

.................................................................................

.................................................................................

.................................................................................

.................................................................................

.................................................................................

.................................................................................

*If anyone is in Christ, he is a new creation. The old
has passed away; behold, the new has come.*

2 CORINTHIANS 5:17 ESV

Many people know or have heard the Serenity Prayer. The prayer generally goes as follows: "God, grant me the serenity to accept the things I cannot change, the courage to change the things I can, and the wisdom to know the difference." This prayer has been adopted by Alcoholics Anonymous and other twelve-step programs, but it is universally applicable. It is a prayer that focuses on a desperate desire for change from the negative to the positive and an appeal for wisdom. The Bible reveals that spiritual change will come when you are in Christ. But situational and other changes require prayer.

You grow a little wiser every day when you take time to evaluate and learn from your experiences. There will always be some things you cannot change. Likewise, there will always be things you can change. Wisdom helps you know the difference.

Take time to pray about the things you can change. Then map out a direction for that change and the self-improvements you hope to make. You will find there is plenty of work ahead, work that will yield good results. As you change within, you will change your attitude. You will have peace knowing you are always striving to improve.

*Lord, give me the wisdom and courage I need to make necessary changes to improve.*

*Wounds from a friend can be trusted, but*
*an enemy multiplies kisses.*

PROVERBS 27:6

Actions reveal who truly loves you. People who pretend to care but hurt you or jealously compete with you are called *frenemies*. Their deceptive care and concern can be your downfall. But you do not need them and can let go of such relationships.

In the book of Proverbs, King Solomon gave sound advice to his son about this type of friendship. He implied that an enemy under the guise of being a friend may do everything right but has an ulterior motive. This enemy selfishly seeks to take something you have, hurt you, or worse, destroy your hope. Solomon advised that you learn to recognize your frenemies and seek out friends who have your best interests at heart.

Real friends will be honest with you even though the truth may hurt. Real friends also encourage you to reach your goals, commiserate with you over disappointments, and want to spend quality time with you. Genuine friends are truly happy, with no displays of jealousy when you succeed. Be thankful when a friend responds with joy over your good news or hugs you when you share bad news. Furthermore, learn to be the kind of friend you want to find.

*Father, thank You for the real friends You have brought into my life. Help me to be a real friend too.*

*As for you, be strong and do not give up,*
*for your work will be rewarded.*

2 Chronicles 15:7

Have you ever had a project that needed to be completed but was so tiring, long, or drawn out that you didn't think you could keep going one more minute? You may have taken a deep breath or rested a few minutes, but then you continued on because you had to complete the task. You overcame the desire to quit.

The Israelites had a desire to build a temple for God, but it was a long process. It took forty-six years for the temple to be built (John 2:20). The temple began with David, who first desired to build the temple, and although he was not the one to build it, when it was finished, it staggered the imagination with its magnificence. Among other stately features, its walls and floor were overlaid with gold, and there was a great celebration at its completion.

Have you invested a lot into a hope or dream and not seen results yet? Do you wonder whether it is time to give up, time to invest a little more effort, or almost time for the goal to be realized? The choice should be not to give up. Seeing your work to its completion will be a reward in itself. Focus on taking one more step forward.

...................................................................

*Lord, when I grow weary from working toward my goal and I am unsure if I will ever see results, give me strength to take one more step.*

*Blessed is the one whose transgressions are*
*forgiven, whose sins are covered.*

PSALM 32:1

It is easy to pass on dejection to others by being grumpy or unkind. It is also easy to push to get your way and sulk if you do not get your way. Essentially, it is easy to hurt other people. However, it is a blessing to be forgiven for these offenses and to forgive others.

Jesus taught His disciples about forgiveness. On one occasion Peter questioned Jesus about how many times a person should be forgiven. Peter then asked if forgiving seven times was enough. Jesus responded, "I tell you, not seven times, but seventy-seven times" (Matthew 18:22). Jesus wanted Peter, and us, to know that we should never keep count of the number of times we forgive someone, and we should always forgive those who sincerely ask for forgiveness and desire to show they have changed their ways.

Each evening, ask yourself if your actions and words may have hurt someone. Be quick to ask for forgiveness or send a note to apologize. Also, forgive anyone who slights you, with the hope that you will be forgiven for your offenses. Be thankful when you are forgiven.

...........................................................................

*Dear Father, thank You for the forgiveness that is available to me because of Jesus. Help me forgive others and quickly ask for forgiveness when I have caused hurt.*

*After you have suffered a little while, the God of all grace,*
*who has called you to his eternal glory in Christ, will*
*himself restore, confirm, strengthen, and establish you.*

I Peter 5:10 esv

We all experience different seasons throughout our lives—seasons of joy and celebration, of grief and despair, and of waiting and receiving. Some seem to pass by in an instant, like a teenager's high school years, while others seem to go on forever, like those middle-of-the-night infant feedings. You may not be in the season you desire right now, but you can still find rest where you are.

As moms, we tend to always be looking forward—to the next age and stage, the next developmental milestone, the next financial responsibility to save for. If you're in a season of suffering or sadness, you're hoping for a season of relief and celebration. But sometimes the Lord asks you to stay in a difficult season, which can feel exhausting. Yet, dear mama, He will give you a reprieve.

God's plan, though you may not understand it, is perfectly thought out. There is a reason you're in this place at this time. Rest in the knowledge that the Lord is right there beside you. And He's telling you, "I am in control. Don't be afraid." You can trust His plan.

......................................................................

*God, thank You for being with me through every season of life and mother-*
*hood, both in the heights of joy and in the depths of sadness.*

*Keep me safe, my God, for in you I take refuge.*

PSALM 16:1

I'm home" are words that echo through a house when a loved one returns home from a trip or after work. It is a warm greeting of joy that waits for a response. Too often loneliness replaces homecomings. A home is a refuge where we are surrounded by love and family. In the Bible, David sometimes referred to God as his refuge. David had learned from difficult experiences that he could always go to God for safety and care.

After the loss of a loved one or a broken relationship, there is an empty feeling, much like a hollowness, that echoes in your soul. Reaching out to connect with someone else may fill the emptiness for a time. But reaching out to God as your refuge will revive your hope.

With the use of the internet, many people are less connected in person, but we still long for face-to-face interaction as a way to connect with others. If you are experiencing this emptiness, you may benefit from volunteering or joining a group where you will find people in need of hugs or warm words. As you create new relationships and invite others into your life, you will find new hope. And when you go to God, He will take you in. He is your refuge and will keep you safe.

...............................................................................

*Dear Father, You are my refuge and my strength. Thank You for awakening my hope.*

*But those who hope in the LORD will renew their strength.*

ISAIAH 40:31

Have you felt a bit weary or overwhelmed lately? Life gets busy, and sometimes dreams get lost in the daily routine.

The prophet Isaiah offered encouragement to people whose dreams had faded right before their eyes. The people of Judah had spent seventy years in captivity, and Isaiah helped them to see that their Creator, God, had not abandoned them. They thought that God had forgotten about them, but Isaiah said that God knows everything that He has created by name, so how could He forget His people? Isaiah encouraged them to focus on God and open their eyes to what they already knew about Him. God is strong and powerful, and He equips people with His power when they need it.

When you take a break and spend time with just yourself and God, you allow yourself to rest and be refreshed. Calm your spirit and revitalize your tired body with a long, hot bath, or bask in a sunset as you let the failures and commotion dissolve from your mind. Pray and reflect on God and your favorite Scripture verses to renew your soul. When your hope is in Him, He will renew your energy and prepare you to tackle whatever is next.

...................................................................

*Dear Father, You are a powerful and strong God. Thank You for renewing my energy when I become weak.*

........................................................................

........................................................................

........................................................................

........................................................................

........................................................................

........................................................................

........................................................................

........................................................................

........................................................................

........................................................................

........................................................................

........................................................................

........................................................................

........................................................................

........................................................................

........................................................................

........................................................................

........................................................................

*While they were eating, Jesus took bread, and when*
*he had given thanks, he broke it and gave it to his*
*disciples, saying, "Take it; this is my body."*

MARK 14:22

On more than one occasion Jesus took bread, prayed, broke the bread, and fed a crowd of people. One occasion was the miracle of feeding the crowds with fish and loaves (Mark 8:1–8). On another occasion, He took bread, broke it, and gave it to His disciples as a symbol of His broken body. This instance was symbolic because Jesus also knew that His disciple Judas would betray Him, and then His body would be beaten, broken, and hung on the cross for us. Three days later Jesus rose from the grave so that we could have eternal life. His brokenness is our salvation.

God uses brokenness to reveal His glory. When Paul suffered from some form of affliction, He asked God to remove it from his life. But God said, "My grace is sufficient for you, for my power is made perfect in weakness" (2 Corinthians 12:9).

We are not perfect, but God will use our imperfections to point to His perfect grace and love. Give God what is broken in your life and pray that He will use the brokenness to bring great hope.

.....................................................................

*Dear God, I have been broken so many times and in so many ways. Use my*
*brokenness to bless others with hope.*

..............................................................................

..............................................................................

..............................................................................

..............................................................................

..............................................................................

..............................................................................

..............................................................................

..............................................................................

..............................................................................

..............................................................................

..............................................................................

..............................................................................

..............................................................................

..............................................................................

..............................................................................

..............................................................................

..............................................................................

..............................................................................

..............................................................................

..............................................................................

*You gave abundant showers, O God; you*
*refreshed your weary inheritance.*

Psalm 68:9

Is your heart downcast? Why do you feel troubled? This world has so much heartache. Our families carry wounds, friends let us down, loved ones pass away, and it may seem as if life is too hard to handle. We live in a broken world. And we love among broken people.

Perhaps today you are trying your best to fight against despair, but your prayers feel heavy. The weight of this struggle is dragging you down—and you're not sure if you have enough strength to get back up. You feel tired and discouraged.

Take heart, for the Lord will rescue you. You can let that burden slide off your back; He promises to carry your heartache, your shame, and your sorrows. In the middle of this storm, remember that God promises to never leave or forsake you—and He means it. Find rest, dear one, in Christ alone.

..................................................................

*Lord, I'm no match for this life's trials. Please give me rest and comfort me with Your presence.*

*Submit to God and be at peace with him.*

JOB 22:21

W e live in an information-saturated world. All we need to do is type something into an internet search bar, and a plethora of information appears at our fingertips. If you wonder what koalas eat or if you want to know the early signs of Alzheimer's disease, that information is just a few clicks on the keyboard away. As a culture, we have become addicted to information, and we seek it out daily.

Sometimes, however, we need rest from that information overload. Our brains are bombarded with information all day long, from ads that pop up in our browsers to texts about impending bad weather. What would it look like for you to rest from seeking information today?

Ask God to help you be at rest with unanswered questions today. After all, do you really need to know right this second what koalas eat? Give your mind some rest, and allow yourself the refreshment of just being.

...............................................................................

*When my mind is overloaded with information, Lord, remind me to seek*
*You and Your kingdom first.*

........................................................................

........................................................................

........................................................................

........................................................................

........................................................................

........................................................................

........................................................................

........................................................................

........................................................................

........................................................................

........................................................................

........................................................................

........................................................................

........................................................................

........................................................................

........................................................................

........................................................................

........................................................................

........................................................................

........................................................................

*"God blesses those who work for peace, for they
will be called the children of God."*

MATTHEW 5:9 NLT

Have you ever noticed a physical reaction when you're worried?
For many, a pounding heart; sweating, shaky hands; shortness of
breath; difficulty swallowing; nausea; and dizziness begin to take hold
of the body. It may not be obvious at first, but as your worries increase,
the physical symptoms become stronger.

Have you felt any of those things this week? Do you feel surprised
by how well those symptoms describe you? If so, your body is trying to
get your attention. Take a moment to listen: mama, this life has many
worries, but our God is bigger and stronger than them all.

Take a deep breath. As you breathe in, remind yourself of God's
promises and faithfulness. As you breathe out, imagine all your worries
flowing out of your body—because where the Spirit of the Lord is,
there is freedom and no place for worry. Continue this deep breathing
until your body relaxes and the Lord calms you. God is bigger than any
trouble or worry; ask Him to fill you with His spirit of peace.

......................................................................

*God, I'm full of worry, but I know You're able to take this from me.*

*Peter got out of the boat and walked on
the water and came to Jesus.*
MATTHEW 14:29 ESV

A s the months and years fly past, you soon recognize that life is too short. Allow this knowledge of the brevity of life to help you live with intention. If you choose to spend time doing what matters—investing in your children, growing in your faith, nurturing relationships—you're well on your way to living a meaningful life.

Do you intentionally arrange your schedule so that there is time for those things that matter most and those things that interest you? Do you make decisions to invest your hours in what feeds your purpose?

Peter was the disciple most likely to act on his passions, for good or ill. If anyone was going to get out of the boat when they saw the potential of walking on water, it would be him. Some critique Peter's moment because he began to sink due to a lack of faith. But Jesus may have also appreciated Peter's zeal and earnest desire to join Him in His miracle.

The apostle Paul wrote that our works were "prepared beforehand, that we should walk in them" (Ephesians 2:10 ESV). It changes our whole perspective when we realize they have been waiting for us. They are gifts God wrapped up for us that are delivered when He calls us forth; we find them when we choose to pursue a purposeful life.

..............................................................................

*Dear God, help me to live an intentional life by walking in the works You
have prepared for me.*

........................................................................

........................................................................

........................................................................

........................................................................

........................................................................

........................................................................

........................................................................

........................................................................

........................................................................

........................................................................

........................................................................

........................................................................

........................................................................

........................................................................

........................................................................

........................................................................

........................................................................

........................................................................

*I consider my life worth nothing to me; my only aim is to*
*finish the race and complete the task the Lord Jesus has given*
*me—the task of testifying to the good news of God's grace.*

ACTS 20:24

Life is full of beautiful things: vibrant sunflowers, a perfect ball game, sunsets, bluebirds, and birch trees; loving friendships, good books, delicious food, and quiet moments of stillness. And sometimes, it's tempting to show others only the beautiful things in our lives. To present the perfect picture, we push the clutter out of the way, suck in our stomachs, throw the dishes in the dishwasher, or stash the miscellaneous piles in a closet. We don't want others to know about the messy parts.

Because while life is beautiful, it's also messy. And we all have our own messes—our own secrets, dirty laundry (real *and* metaphorical!), and less-than-perfect pasts. The good news is this: God can turn messy into beautiful. That's what He's best at. You don't have to have it all together. It's okay that your life is less than picture-perfect.

Rely on the Lord, and rest in Him. You don't have to hide your brokenness from Him, and He doesn't want you to. Not only can He mend it, but He can also transform it into something beautiful.

..................................................................................

*Father, thank You for sending Jesus to turn the messy, sinful parts of my*
*life into something beautiful.*